TAO OF
CHINESE TEA

A CULTURAL AND PRACTICAL GUIDE

LING YUN

The Reader's Digest Association, Inc.
Pleasantville, New York / Montreal / Sydney

FOR SHANGHAI PRESS & PUBLISHING DEVELOPMENT COMPANY
Text: Ling Yun
Photographs provided by Ling Yun and ImagineChina
Interior and Cover Designer: Wang Wei
Assistant Editor: He Siyuan
Editor: Yang Xinci, Anna Nguyen
Editorial Director: Wu Ying
President and Publisher: Wang Youbu

Library of Congress Cataloging-in-Publication Data
Yun, Ling, 1976-
    Tao of Chinese tea : a cultural and practical guide / Ling Yun.
      p. cm.
    Includes bibliographical references and index.
    ISBN 978-1-60652-050-5
1. Tea—Social aspects—China. 2. Tea—China—History. 3. Chinese tea ceremony. 4. Drinking customs
—China—History. 5. China—Social life and customs. I. Title.
GT2907.C6Y855 2009
394.1'20951—dc22
                                                                                        2009019873

We are committed to both the quality of our products and the service we provide to our customers. We value
your comments, so please feel free to contact us:
    The Reader's Digest Association, Inc.
    Adult Trade Publishing
    Reader's Digest Road
    Pleasantville, NY 10570-7000

For more Reader's Digest products and information, visit our website:
    www.rd.com (in the United States)
    www.readersdigest.ca (in Canada)]
    www.readersdigest.co.uk (in the UK)
    www.readersdigest.com.au (in Australia)
    www.readersdigest.com.nz (in New Zealand)
    www.rdasia.com (in Asia)

THE READER'S DIGEST ASSOCIATION, INC.
President and Chief Executive Officer: Mary Berner
President of Asia Pacific: Paul Heath
President and Publisher, U.S. Trade Publishing: Harold Clarke

Printed in China by Shanghai Donnelley Printing Co. Ltd.

1 3 5 7 9 10 8 6 4 2

Contents

Fine teas are strongly recommended because of their positive health benefits.

The Health Benefits of Chinese Tea

More than a widely-consumed beverage in the world, tea is a friend for Zen meditation that helps us gain inner peace. Besides, fine teas, hot or over ice, are strongly recommended because of their positive health benefits. A medical book from the Tang dynasty over one thousand years ago said, "Tea cures every disease." It may sound a little bit exaggerated. The Chinese, however, have been using tea for thousands of years for its different effects such as weight loss, lowering blood pressure, the prevention of cancers and curing stress-related diseases.

Modern science illustrates that tea has a very low fat and caloric content as well as containing plenty of protein and vitamins. Tea leaves are a rich natural source of polyphenolic antioxidant catechins (often incorrectly referred to as tannins), aromatic or essential oils and caffeine. The polyphenol is the most important element because it provides the greatest positive health benefit through a quite complex mechanism.

Kills Bacteria

Tea's medicinal properties are not a new discovery. Legend recalls that a renowned Chinese ancestor, Shen Nong, who lived more than 5,000 years ago, ate tea leaves if he tasted poisonous herbs during the collection of vegetable and herbal medicines. He was regarded as the God of Agriculture. This story indicates that tea was first used as an amazing healer instead of a beverage when humans found it. According to various ancient Chinese medical books, tea liquid can cure hepatitis, dysentery as well as enteritis. Today, there is still a tradition in China where brewed tea leaves are placed on small wounds, inflamed gums or red swollen eyes to speed recovery. All kinds of teas, especially green tea, black tea and Oolong, have been linked to the control of diarrhea and inhibiting unhealthy bacterial cell growth such as Salmonella, while promoting healthy stomach bacterial growth.

Aids Digestion

After tea became nationally fashionable during the Tang dynasty, tea drinking was accordingly introduced to ethnic minorities and foreign countries

Tea served during the ancient Chinese banquet

as the essence of a civilized way of living. While learning The Chinese Tao of Tea, the Koryo State, a neighboring country of China, explained in their records why tea was tremendously popular: "People of the Tang Empire all ate meat. Whereas tea served as a way to improve digestion and in turn, eliminate jaundice (a traditional Chinese medical term, which referred to the discomforts brought on by eating plenty of meats). In areas of Tibet, Xinjiang and Mongolia where inhabitants eat beef, mutton, butter and cheese as their staple foods, there is a saying 'Can't live without tea, even for a day'."

Fights Aging

Aging is natural for all humans. Many people these days, especially women, are eager to find the best anti-aging products such as anti-wrinkle cream or drugs in order to turn back the hands of time. Actually, several medical research studies show that green tea can play a huge role in helping them do it. It is because green tea leaves contain a very powerful antioxidant called polyphenolic catechins, which can lower the amount of DNA damaging free radicals in the body. Catechin, which is not found in coffee, has an anti-oxidation function 40 to 100 times stronger than vitamin C. Not all teas contain the same amount of catechins. Non-fermented green teas such as Longjing retain many more catechins than semi-fermented teas such as Oolong. The fully fermented black teas have the least amount of catechins. Furthermore, polyphenolic catechins may reduce the risk of age-related degenerative brain disorders such as Alzheimer disease. The Chinese deeply believe that tea helps them live much longer. For example, figures like Emperor Qianlong (1711-1799) of the Qing dynasty, one of the most successful rulers in the history of China, said that the key to his regimen was tea. So, like all the long-living persons, he insisted on drinking tea every day of his life.

Assists Weight Loss

Tea helps the body lose weight by burning more calories, according to the studies from *The American Journal of Clinical Nutrition* in 1999. From my first-hand experience, Oolong tea and Pu'er tea seem to have the most

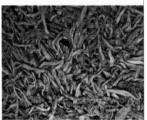

Pu'er tea, which can help someone stay slim, can be divided into "raw"(top) and "crusted" (bottom) types. Fresh made Pu'er tea called "raw" is often wild and untamable in its herbal nature. Once it turns into older crusted tea, it becomes gentler for the stomach. So the latter is more suitable for those new to drinking Pu'er.

significant results among all the six basic categories of tea. When looking at most other tea supplements on the market, they are both often used as an ingredient in many diet products, especially in France and Japan. A study of the impact of water, green tea and Oolong on the Basal Metabolic Rate (BMR), a rate the body metabolizes energy, found tea could affect the BMR. Water has no particular function on BMR. Green tea can raise 4 calories of the BMR per hour, while Oolong can raise it by 9 calories. The function of this can last up to five hours. In other words, only one cup of 300cc Oolong tea can burn 40 calories. This is equivalent to fast walking for 15 minutes or climbing stairs for 10 minutes.

Prevents Cancer

Tea helps your body lose weight by burning more calories, according to the studies.

Another study was designed to investigate the effects of two main constituents of green tea, EGCG (Epi-Gallo-Catechin-Gallate) and caffeine, on intestinal tumorigenesis in Apcmin/+ mice, a recognized mouse model for human intestinal cancer, and to elucidate possible mechanisms involved in the inhibitory action of the active constituent (Cancer Res. Vol.65 pp. 10623-10631 & Biol. Pharm. Bull. Vol.30 pp. 200-204). Another study done by the University of Purdue has found that there is a compound present in green tea that stops cancer cells from growing. Also, research conducted in 1998 suggested that men who drank three cups of green tea a day were 30 percent less likely to develop prostrate cancer.

Lowers Blood Pressure & Protects the Heart

The antioxidant substances flavonoid and EGCG in tea, may delay the development of hypertension and reduce blood pressure. In a population study with Norwegian men and women, higher intake of black tea was linked to a lower systolic blood pressure in the cohort. In a study on men and women above age 20, in comparison to those who did not drink tea, the risk of hypertension went down 46 percent in those who drank 2-3 cups of tea per day, and 65 percent in those drinking more than 3 cups per day. Another study showed the same favourable effects of tea consumption on systolic and diastolic blood pressure in older women.

The health effect of EGCG helps to lower the bad cholesterol (LDL) by an average of 10 percent and improved the ratio between LDL and the good caholesterol (HDL). Where dangerous cholesterol has already stuck to the artery, flavornoid helps to prevent it from damaging the inner lining. Tea protects against heart disease by preventing the hypertrophy of one's heart, which can stop blood from forming abnormal clots that could cause heart attacks and strokes (Drug Metab. Dispos. Vol.16 pp.98-103). The process of this mechanism is like water flowing more smoothly after the build-up has been removed from old pipes.

Treats Colds and Flu

Asian people have long used white tea to eliminate fever in children who exhibit symptoms of cold and flu viruses. You can also simply drink green tea because its EGCG can cause the inhibition of the hemagglutinin and the neuraminidase, the two transmission tools of flu (Antiviral Res. Vol.68 pp66-74). I drink tea a few times daily in the early spring and winter to boost my immunity, adding a slice of lemon in a cup of black tea with a ½ teaspoon of mint. If you are sick, you will notice a gradual decrease of your influenza by drinking tea. A drop of honey in a cup of black tea also eases a sore throat. This therapy is better than drinking warm water mixed with salt.

Protects from the Harm of Electromagnetic Radiation

Protection from radiation is a unique effect of tea. In modern times, electromagnetic radiation is everywhere. In the office, there are computers, photocopiers, laser printers and fax machines. At all times, cell phones are always near by whether you're using yours or someone is using one right next to you. Back at home, there are still microwaves, ovens as well as televisions. Both epicatechin and vitamins are present in significant quantities in green tea. It is known that these compounds are able to inhibit the oxidation of radiation harm. For couch potatoes, take a cup of tea while watching TV.

Refreshes Oneself

Caffeine may not be so bad. When the legendary Shen Nong and Bodhi-Dharma tasted tea, each was exhilarated to find that it cleared their minds. The amount of caffeine in green tea (about 20mg/150ml) is much less than coffee (about 100mg/150ml). Drinking a cup of green tea is helpful in your recovery after working overnight.

Other Health Benefits

In addition to the above effects, the consumption of tea has been shown to

Tea protects you from the harm of electromagnetic radiation as its unique effect in modern times.

Tea always refreshes yourself.

have many other health benefits. These include:

Tooth care: Tea can reduce the amount of plaque on the teeth by killing the bacteria that forms it. Galconoid in tea also helps to fight cavities by stopping bacteria from sticking to the teeth. The traditional Chinese would clean their mouths and teeth by gargling with tea after getting up every morning.

Builds the bone: Falconoid, found in tea protects the bones.

Diabetes Tea is able to influence the body's sensitivity to insulin and affects glucose tolerance levels.

Fights UV light: Catechin plays a role in the prevention of skin cancers and is thought to be able to protect the skin from ultra violet radiation.

Anything to Avoid?

Due to its caffeine content, tea should be avoided by infants, young children and those who have lost sleep. Pregnant and breastfeeding women should drink tea in limited amounts.

For individuals who feel nauseated while drinking tea without milk, it's best to eat something small such as half of a biscuit. For people required to follow a caffeine free diet, the quantities of caffeine in both green and black (about 55mg/150ml) teas are significant. Those with a stomach-ache should drink tea after meals.

You might be pleasantly surprised by how much better you'll feel by drinking tea. After taking a sip, let's explore its Zen-like qualities of calmness and harmony and the stories behind it.

Tea culture is an integral part of life for the Chinese people.

Introduction

A Tea Cup of Oriental Wisdom

If you are as fond of Chinese Kung Fu as I am, you may notice that the concept of Wu Xing (five elements) is highly stressed in the martial art. The ability to master Wu Xing can determine if a student will go on to become the next Bruce Lee, Jackie Chan or Jet Li. Wu Xing refers to the integration of the five elements: metal, wood, earth, water and fire. Then, why is Wu Xing so emphasized? Ancient Chinese scholars thought that these elements were fundamental to the world. Everything in the universe, from the numerous galaxies to the tiniest particles, contains some quantity of all the five elements. Once you understand Wu Xing, you can seize the basic principles of Chinese culture.

Naturally, Chinese tea is no exception when it comes to following the principles of Wu Xing. To illustrate, the element of metal expresses the spirit of tea, including China's Tao, history and conventions. In China's Tao, metal has the meaning of "convergence and cleaning," which infers that the trace element contents of tea leaves could do detoxification benefits to human body after the process of tea producing. Wood is related to the properties of this kind of plant, such as the species and effect on health. The earth represents the materials used to craft tea sets like *Zisha* pots and porcelain *gaiwan* (cover-bowl cup). The water, is used to

Tea is a friend for Zen meditation to gain our inner peace.

moisten the tea leaves. The last element fire is used in its production and gives the fresh leaves their shape. Understanding the Wu Xing of Chinese tea is like knowing the pet peeves, zodiac, hobbies and birth place of a friend. Through my pen and photography, this book will give you a greater appreciation into the art of tea, from its legendary history to discovering its many varieties. It's also a useful guide on how to find and savour Chinese tea in the comforts of your home.

There is an age-old Chinese saying that reveals the importance of tea in daily life, "When the door is opened every day, seven things are necessary for the family: firewood, rice, oil, salt, soy sauce, vinegar and tea." The Chinese regarded tea as a daily necessity along with the essential seasonings of their vibrant cuisine. Lin Yutang, a famous writer once commented, "With a teapot, a Chinese is happy wherever he/she goes." On the other hand, the well-educated and sophisticated ancient Chinese considered "lute-playing, chess, calligraphy, painting, poem, opera and tea art" as the seven landmark artistic skills that they must acquire. The core of Oriental culture is demonstrated in the process of tea-making, from the boiling to the drinking ceremony, as well as the delicate philosophy behind it.

Consequently, tea has suited both refined and popular tastes and found its way deep into the heart of the Chinese people. For many Westerners, it is not until they arrive in China that they realize that an invitation to drink tea actually means a business talk or an opportunity for relationship building. In some areas in China, it is said that about half of the business deals are accomplished in tea houses.

The Chinese Tao of Tea, the philosophy of tea, first appeared in the Chinese poem of the Tang dynasty more than one thousand years ago. Then it was introduced to Japan and became known as さどう (Teaism). The Chinese do not sip and taste tea simply as a social activity or a way to maintain health , but as a life-long cultivation of morality, temperament and aesthetic appreciation. Imagine that for the past five thousand years without film, newspaper or internet, tea culture has been successfully passed down from one generation to the next, by word of mouth or with the brush pens of several famous historic figures. Traditions are passed down orally from one tea master to the next. Such crystallization of wisdom not only reflects the Chinese philosophies of Confucianism and Taoism, but also embraces the essence of Buddhism which was later introduced into China. Therefore, tea drinking can be regarded as a representation of the Oriental culture for its worship of art, love for peace and pursuit of harmony.

Tea culture is an integral part of life for the Chinese people. The love for the Chinese Tao of Tea has long been deemed as an elegant hobby full of enjoyment. Most of the time, the Chinese Tao of Tea is unwritten among the Chinese people. As time has passed by, even some modern Chinese do not understand this philosophical system though tea drinking remains popular in contemporary society. The Chinese would describe this as "admiring a flower in a fog", unable to truly see it.

How then, do the Chinese use tea to express deep meaning with sublime words? There is a story as an illustration.

A young man who failed repeatedly in life came to an accomplished monk and asked in frustration, "Where's the hope for a miserable loser like me to go on living?"

The monk said nothing after hearing his words, except telling a little sramanera, a Buddhist novice, to boil some warm water to greet the young man from afar.

A moment later, the little sramanera came back with a kettle in hand. The old monk picked up a handful of tea, dropped it into a cup, steeped it in warm water, and put it in front of the guest, saying, "Please have some tea."

Tasting the tea, the young man shook his head, "What tea is this? It's scentless!"

"It's Tie Guan Yin (a very famous Chinese Oolong tea). How can it be scentless?" said the monk, who was smiling. He then asked the little sramanera to bring a kettle of boiled water.

This time, he brewed the leaves with the hot water. Within moments, the scent of the delicate tea tinged the air of the room. The young man could not help taking the cup up.

"It's the same tea, but smells different. Do you have any idea why?" asked the monk. The young man thought for a while and answered, "It must be due to the different temperature. One cup was brewed by hot water, while the other by warm water."

"Exactly. Different water temperature determines the scent. If you brew

Ancient temple on the remote mountain

tea with warm water, the tea leaves can only float over the surface. In that case, how can it emit its entire potential aroma? Instead, if you brew with boiled water for a couple of times, the tea leaves moving up and down can release the mildness of the spring rain, the hotness of the summer sunshine, the mellowness of the autumn wind, and the coolness of the winter frost. "

Upon hearing the monk's words, the young man had a sudden awakening: Life is like the tea story. Pains and setbacks, gains and successes are inevitable during our careers, study and love life. Life can not be full if you do not conquer your suffering.

Generally, the Chinese Tao of Tea is like *The Canterbury Tales* for they

Five chapters of this book bring you deep insights of Tao of Chinese tea.

both teach wisdom about life in a way that's easy to understand. I hope that the readers of this book can not only learn more about the tea in Chinese history, but also its close connection with contemporary China today.

In the first chapter "Metal," you will meet China's most famous elite such as its emperors and artists. They indulged so much in tea that they wrote numerous poems and books about it, planted it, and became recognized tea masters. You'll learn why the well-known emperor of the Song dynasty, Song Huizong, performed tea ceremonies before his minister officials, and why the greatest poet in the Tang dynasty, Li Bai (701-762 AD), was willing to become a spokesman for a certain kind of green tea? You'll also find out how Confucianism, Taoism and Zennism inspired diverse tea customs and etiquettes.

After being immersed in the spirit of Chinese tea, the third and the fourth chapters serve as practical and handy reference for brewing, including how to choose and use tea utensils, and the documentaries of tea ceremonies performed by China's best tea master. Utensils is a professional phrase used by tea masters to describe all teaware including the tea pot and tea tray. Whatever you watch or take part in, you will receive enjoyment of art appreciation along with pressure deduction.

When you go to buy tea, chapter two offers lists of popular teas and chapter five gives you the golden rules for "Dos or Don'ts." The selection of tea is an art within itself.

In short, this book is a must-have companion for readers who have interest in Chinese tea and the rich Oriental tradition behind it. Well, let us start our date with tea right now.

METAL

The royal golden tea sets from the Tang dynasty in the Famen Temple of Shaanxi Province

CHAPTER ONE
METAL

1. The Classic Stories of Tea: History & Customs

With the prologue "History became legend, legend became myth," taken from *The Lord of the Rings*, we track down the footsteps of Chinese tea to uncover the truths about its origins from the very beginning.

The Chinese character "Tea" written with calligraphic brush

Why the Name Tea?
Are "Cha," "Tay," "Tea" Really the Same?

Some Westerners may be puzzled that tea is actually pronounced "cha" in Mandarin, the national language of the country. The pronunciation of "tea" actually comes from a different Chinese dialect. In Mandarin and Cantonese, it is pronounced "cha"; while in Fukienese (a dialect of South Fujian Province), it is "tay." Both of these names spread to the rest of the world.

For instance, in the last year of the Ming dynasty (1644), British merchants came to trade at Xiamen Port, where the Chinese tea was called "tay," and they spelled it as "tea." So "tea" later became widely accepted by the English-speaking world. The French "the," Italian and Spanish "te," Korean "ta" as well as German and Dutch "thee" are also descendants of "tay." Through the route of Persia, "ch'a" in Mandarin came to be "cha" in Japanese and Hindu, "shai" in Arabian as, "chay" in Turkish, and "chai" in Russian.

What is the Truth behind Its Discovery?

Who was the first one to savor the fragrant delicacy of tea? There are at least three totally different stories that make the truth unknown.

The earliest answer to this question comes from a book dating back to the Western Han dynasty (about 206 BC) two thousand years ago, which says, "Shen Nong came across seventy-two toxic herbs daily in tasting hundreds of plants, but took Tu (the name of tea before the Tang dynasty) as an antidote." Shen Nong, who lived 5,000 thousand years ago and taught people farming methods, is regarded in the Chinese folklore as the God of Agriculture. During this time, people often became sick or even died from eating poisonous plants. To help them, Shen Nong decided to taste all plants in the remote mountains in order to tell people what to eat. He placed those edible or useful as healers (the original forms of today's vegetable and herbal medicines) in his left bag and the toxic ones in his right bag. It is said that Shen Nong had a transparent belly, meaning that he could see through his skin to look at whatever he had eaten.

One time during a collection, he came across a toxic herb, which made him dizzy with a dry throat and a numb tongue. He quickly sat down, resting his back on a big tree full of lush green leaves. Shen Nong picked two leaves and chewed on them. Surprisingly, a delicate fragrance rose from this. The leaves he had taken were like doctors curing him off his ailment. Soon, his stomach felt clean as if it had been washed by the leaves. With the liquid under his tongue, he quickly recovered from the discomfort. Thereafter, Shen Nong kept these special leaves in his left bag. He would immediately take the tea leaves if he encountered a poisonous herb.

One day he tasted a fatal herb called "Duanchang Cao" (literally meaning gut breaking herb), which caused his sudden death. Why not eat tea to save himself? This herb was so deadly that Shen Nong did not have the slightest strength to open his bag for tea. Since Shen Nong sacrificed himself for the salvation of mankind, he is recognized as the ancestor of the Chinese nation and one of the three great emperors from ancient times. Today, the Chinese still call themselves "descendants of Yan Di and Huang Di," in which Shen Nong is referred to as Yan Di (Emperor Yan).

A third completely different story says that Bodhi-Dharma, the first patriarch of Chinese Zen, discovered tea. Dharma covered a long distance from India to China to practice Buddhism. He vowed to "face the wall and meditate" for nine years without sleep in a cliff cave near the Shaolin Temple. Outside the cave, there were singing birds and fragrant flowers complimented by an endless vista of natural beauty. But inside, there was only loneliness and darkness. Dharma eventually fell asleep on accident. He was so furious when he woke up that he cut off his eyelids and threw them on the ground nearby. Unexpectedly, a tree grew from where his eyelids lay. Whenever he felt drowsy, Dharma would pick a leaf from the tree to chew to cure his sleepiness. From then on, the refreshing effect of tea leaves gradu-

Portrait of Shen Nong

Another legend sounds more like a version of "Newton's Apple." It says, Shen Nong Clan treated patients by not only collecting herbal medicines, but he also tried them himself first. After Shen Nong collected a large bag of herbs, he set up an iron pot under a tea tree to try them out. He used water from a nearby stream to fill up the pot and started a fire to heat it up. When the water boiled, Shen Nong removed the pot's lid, and turned around to fetch the herbal medicine. A gust of wind then caused several tea leaves to fall into the pot. Shen Nong could immediately smell its delicate fragrance. He took a closer look out of curiosity, and watched the water turn a yellowish green hue. He poured the liquid into a bowl to taste it. With a slight bitterness and fine aroma, it gave a long-lasting pure taste, which satisfied the thirst, refreshed the body, and gradually, cleared the mind. Shen Nong was exhilarated by the discovery.

It is said that Shen Nong was the first one to savor the fragrant delicacy of tea in the world.

ally spread.

Which One of the Three Stories Is the Closest to the Truth?

The legend says Dharma came to China in the Six Dynasties, while written records and archaeological evidence of tea already existed in the Han dynasty, hundreds of years earlier than his arrival. Had Dharma flown through a time tunnel like Harry Potter? In my opinion, the reason why this story circulates, especially in Japan and India, comes from the introduction of tea culture into these two countries with a strong Buddhist influence. This offers an explanation of why Bodhi-Dharma was regarded as the "father of tea".

While the first two stories enjoy widespread popularity, I should also indicate that Shen Nong is actually a representative of the Chinese ancestors in folklore. Although all those discoveries and inventions are attributed to him, they are in essence the embodiment of the collective wisdom of the people at that time (about 2737 BC).

Additionally, I have inspected the wild tea trees as told in the Shen Nong legend. Their offspring still live among the primeval forests of Southwest China, i.e. Yunnan, Sichuan and Guizhou Provinces. Distinguished from the one-meter-tall tea trees that we usually see in tea gardens, the 2,000 to 3,000-year-old wild trees are even higher than a ten-floor building, with their roots grounded deeply into the earth. While the trees raise their heads, they seem to have the power to chat with the stars in the velvet-like sky. For this reason, local villagers prostrate themselves in worship to these big wild tea trees…

These legends show that the medicinal functions of tea leaves had already been recognized by the Chinese, as early as in the primitive society during Shen Nong Clan's time.

The Tea Trade: Bringing Tea to the Masses during the Han Dynasty

After its discovery, tea was restricted to the corner of Southwest China due to the inconvenience of transportation for about 2,400 years.

It was not until 316 BC when the great-great-grandfather of the First

One of the more than 2000-year-old wild tea trees as told in the Shen Nong legend in Ailao Mountain of Yunnan Province

A copper lamp in the shape of a young servant in the Han dynasty

Emperor "Qin Shihuang", King Hui of Qin Kingdom, conquered the small Kingdom of Shu in Sichuan Province that tea was enjoyed by the power elite class. His troops brought tea back to his kingdom in the central area of China, which caused its popularity to grow among the masses.

A story from the Western Han dynasty over two thousand years ago provides evidence that the Chinese middle class already had tea business by 59 BC. Wang Bao, a scholar of *Cifu* (a literary form, sentimental or descriptive composition, often rhymed), used to lodge in a pretty widow's house all through the year. He often asked one of her servants named "Bian Liao" to go shopping for him. Bian Liao was quite reluctant to work for him, regarding Wang as an outsider of his master's family. He was also suspicious about the relationship between Wang and the young mistress.

The servant poured out his grievances at the tomb

Terracotta warriers, discovered in Qin Shihuang's mausoleum, display the strenght of might of the Qin army, whose forefathers brought tea to the central area of China in 316 BC.

of his master and cried, "Master, you only asked me to look after the house. You didn't ask me to go on errands for other men!"

Wang heard the servant's complaints and decided to teach him a lesson. On the Festival of Lanterns, he bought Bian Liao from the young widow.

Unwillingly, Bian Liao became the attendant of Wang Bao. He proposed to Wang that, "Now that you've bought me, you should act like my former master, who stated clearly all my responsibilities in the contract. Otherwise, I won't do it."

Bian Liao seemed to be the first employee in China to ask for a "labor contract."

Wang Bao, with a sense of humor, wrote down a 600-word-long contract jokingly, listing all sorts of labor in great-detail. The agreement occupied every minute of Bian Liao's time from the morning until night, not to mention the weekends and holidays.

The onerous tasks overburdened Bian Liao. In the end, he pleaded to Wang for mercy in tears, "If I work this way any longer, I'm afraid that I'll soon be too exhausted and die from all the work. Had I known this, I would've been happier to buy anything for you everyday." Of course, Bian Liao got a forgiving hand from Wang. Everybody was satisfied and happy.

The relic of this contract tells us that the servant Bian Liao had two duties related to tea. He bought tea from a place called Wu Yang, and cleaned and prepared the tea utensils for Wang. William Ukers, an American scholar, wrote in his famous book *All about Tea* that tea had become an article of trade by the fifth century. However, Wang Bao's contract shows us specialized tea market existed five hundred years before this.

Painting on the brick of drinking tea at a party (Han dynasty)

The Chinese Tao of Tea: At Full Blossom in the Tang Dynasty

In Chinese history, the Tang dynasty brought tea culture into full blossom with its strong national power, prolific creativity and extensive tolerance for great diversity.

Li Bai, often deemed as the greatest Chinese poet, was famous for his verses, "See how the Yellow River's water rushes out of heaven, entering the ocean, never to return." In his long poem "Cactus Tea," he wrote with unflagging patience to describe the tea's birthplace, natural environment, form, quality, taste and healing effect. He also claimed that it could recover one's youthful vigor and bring a rosy complexion. The whole work reads, in my view, just exactly like a complete product description composed by the marketing department of a modern corporation or an AAAA advertising agency. At the end of the poem, he readily proclaimed, "If in the future, the tea is favored by some accomplished monk or hermit, don't forget it is me,

Tea's status as a "national drink" was established during the Tang dynasty.

Li Bai, and my nephew who discovered it!"

During this period, Lu Yu (733-804 AD) also emerged as a ground-breaking figure in the history of the Chinese tea culture. The author of *The Classic of Tea*, later generations honored him as "the Sage of Tea." How did he come to write the world's first tea monograph? In fact, Lu Yu had a legendary life, which began as a discovered orphan. One morning, Zhi Ji, an eminent Tang monk was walking along a lake. Suddenly, he heard a wild goose honking nearby. When he turned towards the goose, he saw an abandoned baby curled up under its wing, shivering in the cold. "Amitabha!" said Zhi Ji, and he quickly carried the baby back to his temple.

In the temple, Lu Yu learned not only how to read, but also the consummate skills of tea-making at an early age because Zhi Ji was an erudite tea lover. At the age of twelve, he escaped the temple and joined a theatrical troupe. Thanks to his wit and talent at performing, Lu Yu had great success as a clown, although he stuttered and looked a bit ugly.

Lu Yu began his journey of tea research at the age of 21. He gathered

A Tang painting of *Lanting Picture Obtained by Xiao Yi* (part) drawn by Yan Liben

tea leaves whenever he came across a mountain and tasted water whenever he came upon a spring. With a pair of cane sandals, he would often walk into the wild on his own to do research. He also met with aged village men who planted the tea to learn more about it. He collected a large amount of tea leaves samples in to study them on his boat. At last, he finished the first draft of his magnum opus on the Chinese Tao of Tea after five years.

In short, *The Classic of Tea* tells everything Lu Yu collected related to tea until the Tang dynasty. Lu Yu believed that "Tea is the drink of gentlemen." The book includes data, including the properties and origins of tea, tea tools, its manufacturing processes, distribution of tea producing areas, techniques in tea-making, different types of water for tea brewing, and drinking methods. The book also had anecdotes like "As a kind of drinks, tea was found by Shen Nong," explained which tea utensils could be omitted on different occasions like being outdoors, and encouraged readers

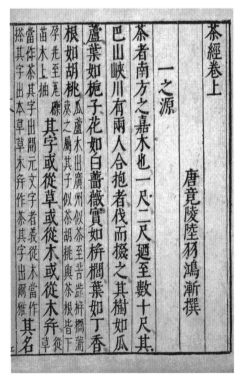

The Classic of Tea written by Lu Yu

to put all the tea activities mentioned in the book into placards, which could be hung in a tea room for a quick reference. The 28 tea utensils created by Lu Yu became such a fad of the time that every wealthy Tang family would keep a complete set.

In a painting from the Tang dynasty, we can see 12 noble ladies drinking tea together. There is a big vessel for holding tea on the center of a large bamboo-surface table. A lady is pouring tea for the others. We can see that people at that time were still using big porcelain bowls instead of cups to drink tea. The ladies are gathered in a relaxed atmosphere, showing their back or front, standing or sitting. They're playing different traditional Chinese musical instruments like a folk music quartet, with a maid playing castanet at one side to match the rhythm, holding a silk fan, listening to music with a bowl in hand, or simply enjoying the tea in graceful manner. In addition, a pup silently rests under the table…

A lady from the Tang dynasty invented the tea bowl with saucer to avoid the hot water from scalding her. This kind of tea set was popular in the following dynasties, which has now become the *gaiwan*.

Revelry in Tang Court from the Tang dynasty

Gold and silver teawares from the Famen Temple in the Tang dynasty

Tea's status as a "national drink" was established during the Tang dynasty. At that time, tea drinking was introduced to ethnic minorities and foreign countries as the essence of a civilized way of living. While learning the Chinese Tao of Tea, the Koryo State, a neighboring country of China, explained why tea drinking was tremendously popular in China in this way: People of the Tang State all ate meat and tea served as a way to eliminate jaundice (traditional Chinese medical terminology, means prevent or cure all kinds of diseases brought by eating plenty of meats). Tea drinks introduced from the Han nationality to Tibet, Xinjiang and Mongolia also received immense attention from the ethnic minorities who ate beef, mutton, butter and cheese as their staple foods. Thus, "Although tea comes from trees in mountain forests, it matters to the government because it influences the national economy."

Tea Art: Another Peak in the Song Dynasty

Tea art reached another peak during the Song dynasty. Zhao Ji, Emperor Huizong of the Song dynasty, was more a gifted artist than an emperor. As an expert in calligraphy, painting and musical instruments, Zhao Ji also had an inexhaustible zest for tea. He was adept in all the popular arts of tea of his time, and had an eye for fine tea utensils. For a better appreciation of the foam from white tea, he highly recommended the black rabbit's hair-patterned cup.

Emperor Huizong is known as the only one among past emperors, that wrote a book about tea. The book, *General Remarks on Tea*, condensed in less than three thousand words, fully elaborates his ingenious ideas on tea. Equally important in the Song dynasty was a highly skillful form of tea art called "various tea games."

Rabbit's hair-patterned cup from the Song dynasty, Jian Kiln

Chaxian (the tea whisk). The leaves were ground to fine powder in a small stone mill, and the preparation was whipped in hot water by a delicate whisk made of split bamboo.

Emperor Huizong was said to have learned it and even performed it in front of the court officials. When playing this game, the player grinds tea into a powder before infusing the utensil with boiling water. Then he whisks the mix with *chaxian* (the tea whisk) to turn the ripples into various patterns representing birds, beasts, insects, fish, flowers or plants, just like ink-wash paintings one after another. They were given the name "paintings in water." A most expert player, for example, could even turn the powder into lines of Tang poems, though they would scatter in an instant. The complicated and redundant procedure merely takes place over a couple of minutes. Therefore, only those experienced with sharp eyes and nimble hands would be able to play it well. Tea drinking differs in the Tang and Song dynasty in that, tea was brewed in Tang while infused in Song. If you want to know how powdered tea is infused, you can read the wonderful work of Zhao Ji.

In *A Decent Party*, a painting drawn by Emperor Huizong, an incense burner is giving out a smoke curling upwards near a grove of trees. Very close lies a *guqin* (an ancient Chinese seven-stringed zither), which awaits for a decent player. The boy servants are infusing tea. The one on the left boils the water. In front of him is a

The form of the Song kettle

Painting of *A Decent Party* drawn by Emperor Huizong from the Song dynasty

charcoal stove with a tea bottle on it. Another boy on the right is scooping tea from a big porcelain jar into a tea bowl. Fruits, snacks and tea cups fully occupy the large table. In the seat, the elegant gentleman in white entertaining the court officials with tea is said to be Emperor Huizong.

It is known that for the Song people, "Tea was an everyday necessity like rice and salt." In the *Scenes along the River during the Qingming Festival*, the genre painting vividly features folk life of the Song dynasty, and the hustle and bustle of the capital Bianjing (today's Kaifeng City of Henan Province) in the Northern Song in great detail. In my eyes, this painting is like a documentary film captured by the ancient Chinese in an era without camera equipment. The whole scroll includes over 550 characters, 60 cattle and 20 wooden boats. Tea houses, taverns, workshops, stores, private residences, and official buildings scatter throughout the painting. An endless stream of horses and carriages flows through the street where men and women from all age groups and all walks of life are shown riding a donkey, shouldering a pole, carrying a sedan chair, or greeting each other, relaxing or strolling about. All together, these people depict the extraordinary commotion and joys of living in this time.

In another close-up shot, let's have a look at the unique "Tea Contest"

Painting of *Scenes along the River during the Qingming Festival* (part) from the Song dynasty

in the Song dynasty. There are four characters, all armed with tea cabinets by their sides. The left one in straw sandals is holding a tea bowl in one hand, and a tea barrel in the other. With a complacent look, he seems to be boasting about his tea. Another one behind him with his sleeves rolled up is pouring the tea from the kettle into the bowl. The two standing on the right side seems to be listening attentively about the features of the tea. This exemplifies that the current tea contest has become part of the social custom. A tea contest requires the powdered tea and water to mix completely together to look like milk. A good tea will leave water marks on the surface of the bowl which called "bite the cup," just like red wine's legs on the edge of glass.

In closing, I want to point out that the main styles of leading Japanese

Painting of *Tea Contest* (part) from the Song dynasty

tea art resemble the Song style. They were based on the tea-making skills that were introduced by the Japanese Monk Yeisai (1131-1215) to his people. Although the Tao of Tea originated in China, many people I meet think that it only exists in Japan instead of China, or if there is such a thing in China, that it was learnted from Japan. In fact, it was generations of Japanese diplomats and monks who came to China to learn the tea cultures during different historical periods from the Tang dynasty to the Ming dynasty, to bring them back to Japan. The black tea bowl from China, for instance, is still a required utensil for today's Japanese ceremonies. It is referred to by its original name "Temmoku", the spelling and pronunciation from the Song dynasty. One thousand years have passed, the Song teaware is still attractive. Furthermore, I am touched by the Japanese attitude towards the Chinese Tao of Tea. They regard the Temmoku tea bowl as the national treasure and deeply bow to it. In order to study tea art, I have also studied the graceful movements of the Japanese

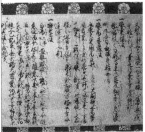

The accomplished Monk Yeisai and his *Keeping Health with Tea*, the first Japanese tea book

Renowned teaware from Japan

tea ceremony. Everytime when my fingers touched the surfaces of the typical Japanese teawares sush as Shino-yaki ware, Oribe-yaki or Rakuyaki tea
bowls, I would be carried away as if seeing the reflection of the Song the
Chinese Tao of Tea in a mirror, like two beautiful flowers blossoming from
the same root.

Reform: The Ming and Qing Dynasties

The founder of the Ming dynasty, Zhu Yuanzhang (1328-1398), issued
a decree to start the use of loose tea, the same tea form as we see today.
Zhu Yuanzhang's grandson ascended the throne after his death. However,
Zhu Di, the uncle of the new emperor, soon launched a four-year war in
order to claim the throne for himself. The whereabouts of the dethroned
emperor were unknown at the time and still remain a mystery. Some evidence shows that Zhu Di assigned Zheng He, his chief eunuch (eunuch,
the male servant who had been castrated and was employed by the emperor), to conduct the great Seven Voyages to the West which eventually

Shadow play

Painting of *Scholars Greeting in a Tea Ceremony* drawn by Wen Zhengming from the Ming dynasty

The classical furniture of both the Ming and early Qing dynasty represents the top quality of Chinese living art. People 400 years ago would sit on such gorgeous chairs to appreciate tea. What a keen enjoyment of life!
(Top: The portable folding chair decorated with *ruyi* and cloud patterns; Bottom: The horseshoe rosewood armchair, both of the Ming style, Huanghuali wood. China Red Sandal Wood Museum collections.)

promoted the export of Chinese tea in the Ming dynasty (as the "Marine Tea Road"). However, it's said that the real purpose of the degree was for Zheng He to find the missing young emperor.

Before the revolt, Zhu Di intimidated his brother Zhu Quan, the 17th son of their father, into supporting the troops and promised to rule the country together with him. Yet after taking the throne, Zhu Di never mentioned the promise again, and the military power of Zhu Quan was also taken away. The betrayal by his brother put Zhu Quan under a great depression. He could express his distraught emotions in traditional opera, *guqin*, calligraphy, and painting. This lord, who fell from the peak of imperial power, gradually came around to become a master of the Chinese Tao of Tea. He wrote his experiences and knowledge into the scroll *A Guide to Tea*, which stated that the purpose of tea art was for the cultivation of morality and temperament from the very beginning. The drinking procedures advocated by Zhu Quan were rid of the fussy traditions. For example, the tea sets were largely reduced to a few minimum as compared with the original "24

A bird's view of the Forbidden City

The study in the Forbidden City built by a tea addict,
Emperor Qianlong, in the Qing dynasty

A thank-you knock

utensils". This reform of tea-drinking six hundred years ago generally led to the modern form of tea-drinking in China.

The form of tea-drinking in the Ming dynasty was followed in the Qing dynasty. As the most longest-living Chinese emperor, Qianlong (1711-1799) believed that the key to his regimen was tea. Four of his six inspection trips to the south, he visited the hometown of "Xihu Longjing". Nowadays, you may see that the Chinese often give a light knock at the tea table or dining table to thank the one serving the tea. It's said that this custom originated from Qianlong. The emperor once had a private inspection in plain clothes in Guangzhou. He entered a tea house accompanied by some court officials. Playing the role of a commoner, the emperor grasped the tea kettle and began to pour tea for the others. The officials all panicked. If they didn't kneel down, they would commit the crime of humiliating the emperor. If they knelt down, they would reveal his identity. In the midst of the emergency, a man suddenly got a good idea to show his gratitude without disclosing the emperor's identity. He curled his index finger and middle finger in a kneeling way and gently knocked the surface of the table, as if showing his gratitude in a small way. Since then, "a thank-you knock" was spread among the people and became a tea convention.

Another story that explains a tea convention also comes from the Qing

The tea house in the Qing dynasty

dynasty. The pampered offspring of Manchu Eight Banners (the noble) often loafed around and created a nuisance wherever they went. These men took bird cages to a tea house with a devious plan to cheat the owner. After finishing the tea, one of them squeezed a bird from a cage into the teapot, and covered it before asking the waiter to refill their water. Ignorant of the swindle, the waiter took the lid off, which allowed the bird to get away. They claimed the waiter freed their rare bird and demanded a high compensation. The host knew that he was blackmailed, yet he had no choice but to pay the men to avoid further trouble. Hence, the tea house took a lesson from this misfortune and made it a rule that any guest requiring water service would need open the pot lid himself. It is still an established custom today. When the water runs out, we don't need to stop the conversation to look for a waiter. We can uncover the lid and place it the side of the teapot for someone to replenish the water.

Clay sculpture of a tea server

Ostindiefararen Götheborg

GÖTHEBORG
12 September
1745

Chinese tea has been exported to Europe since 1610 during the Ming and the Qing dynasties. Recently, Anhui green tea was salvaged from the famous Swedish sunken ship Gothenburg. It is said that, the tea leaves miraculously retained their original color and fragrance from being sealed in white and blue porcelain containers after 260 years.

2. The Spirit of the Chinese Tao of Tea

Tea is the carrier of the Chinese culture, where the values and ideal Tao of the Chinese can be found.

Tao, the most supreme conception of the Chinese philosophies, signifies universal law, ultimate truth, and the general rule governing all motions, or the essence or origin of everything on earth. Mainstream of the Chinese culture used to be the "complementation of Confucianism and Taoism." After the Sui and Tang dynasties, the general trend moved to the "trinity of Confucianism, Zennism and Taoism." Therefore, for Tao, there is the Tao of Confucianism, the Tao of Taoism, and the Tao of Buddhism. None of them are necessarily the same. I heard the Song allegory of the "Three Vinegar Tasters" to explain the development of the three doctrines. Sakyamuni, Confucius, and Laozi (Lao-tzu) once stood before a jar of vinegar—the emblem of life—and each dipped in his finger to taste the brew. The Confucius found the vinegar sour, the Buddha called it bitter, and Laozi pronounced it sweet.

The Chinese Tao of Tea, the philosophy of tea, is also a trinity. The art of tea-drinking aims to cultivate Tao, which comprises the three key fields of tea etiquette, art and Zen. First, tea etiquette refers to the rituals and rules in tea activities. Second, tea art refers to the workmanship with the tea including preparing tea utensils, choosing water, controlling the heat, timing the cooking, and serving the tea. Lastly, tea Zen means to develop temperament, comprehend the truth of Tao and maintain fitness.

Someone has missed the real charm of tea if he takes a careful sip and utters with disappointment, "Oh! It's bitter." He has only experienced its taste without touch-

Tao, the most supreme conception of the Chinese philosophies, signifies universal law, ultimate truth and the essence or origin of everything on earth.

ing the inner spirit of the Chinese Tao of Tea. During its thousands of years' long history, tea has been gradually endowed with a unique cultural value and aesthetic philosophy. Tea signifies politics, culture, economics and even Zen as you'll see in the following philosophies.

Confucianism

The core of Confucianism is etiquette and harmony. For example, the Chinese have the custom "When a guest arrives, a cup of tea will be served." After seating the guest, the host will serve tea as a way to welcome him. During the conversation, tea will add to the friendly at-

Confucius used to be a band conductor. His favorite instrument was the *guqin*, called "the king of Chinese musical instruments." Playing *guqin* and drinking tea is to reach the harmony of body and soul in tranquility. In 2003, UNESCO awarded the art of *guqin* the title "Masterpiece of the Oral and Intangible Heritage of Humanity."

The "thirty percent affection"

mosphere. At the end of the visit, the host raises the tea cup as a way to say it's time for "goodbye."

Another example of Confucianism's philosophy occurs when you enjoy tea at one of today's tea houses in China. You'll find all tea cups only 70% full instead of completely full. The tea house owner or the tea servers will explain to you that this means "Seventy percent tea and thirty percent affection." You may have the same question as me, why not thirty percent tea and seventy percent affection? Why not show more affection? In fact, the "thirty percent affection" explanation is a modern misinterpretation of a tradition that originated from the Han and Tang dynasties. The remaining space in the tea cup means to keep one's mind open, implying the moral of "Pride hurts and modesty benefits." I have heard a story derived from this venerable Chinese philosophy. A respectable Taoist priest received a college professor who came to acquire Tao. After chatting for a few minutes, the priest stood up to serve tea for the guest. The priest filled up the cup, but continued pouring in more tea. "It's full! No tea can be filled in anymore!" cried the professor, who was staring at his cup of overflowing tea. The priest answered, "You are just like the cup of tea, fulfilled by your own judgments, ideas and assumptions in your brain. If the cup is not emptied, how can I reveal the truth of Tao to you?"

Taoism

Tea also contains the wisdom and aesthetics of the Chinese Taoism. Laozi, first named Li Er, was the founder of Taoism. Confucius once returned from a visit to Laozi in Luoyang City and praised him as unfathomable like a dragon flying in clouds, meaning that Laozi was the wisest. Taoism is a way of life which emphasizes the self, accepts the secular, and harmonizes one with the rest of the world. Together with Confucianism, Taoism has become one of the major pillars of the Chinese culture as well.

Similar to Tai-Chi Quan (shadow boxing), also created by the Taoists, Taoism maintains that the art of tea rests with empty quietness, a natural way of doing, and a combination of motion and stillness in the nurturing of a noble spirit.

The famous Tang poem "Thanks to Imperial Counsellor Meng for Sending Me the Freshly Picked Tea" written by Lu Tong (c.775-835) is an ex-

The calligraphy on tea drinking of the Ming dynasty

The cake teas

Painting of *Laozi Riding an Ox*

ample of this belief in tea art (excerpt).

"I am deeply falling asleep during the day time, when a soldier knocks at the door. The gift from a high official, Imperial Counsellor Meng, is packed with white thin silk with seals. Opening the package, I read the letter as if seeing the face of Meng himself. Then after locking the door, I prepare the tea with enjoyment.

"A bowl of tea moistens my lips and throat, while two bowls break the loneliness.

"With three bowls down, the five hundred words of the masterpiece scrolls are the only thing left in mind.

"The fourth bowl sends out gentle sweats of all the wrong and unfairness of life.

"At the fifth bowl I am purified; the sixth makes me feel immortal.

"The seventh one is undrinkable. Alas, I could hardly take anymore! I only feel the wind that breezes under my arms.

"Where is Penglai Mountain, the fabled abode of immortals?

"Let me ride on this wind and fly away."

This tea poem that combines romanticism and realism perfectly! It has struck a chord in the hearts of its readers for more than 1000 years. Even today, many Chinese tea houses or shops still use it as excellent advertisement. Many literators indulge in describing the whole process of tea art—from receiving, cooking, and drinking it to the personal after-taste experiences—because the Chinese Tao of Tea contains the keys to the magical Oriental characteristic of health-preservation.

Zennism

Reading the history of tea, you will see its close relationship to Buddhism from coming across numerous temples and many accomplished monks. The boom of

The painting of *Lu Tong Is Cooking Tea* (by Ding Yunpeng of the Ming dynasty)

tea drinking in the Tang dynasty was indeed a result of the rise of Buddhism, especially Zennism. When learning Zen, one should meditate with the eyes closed. Tea developed into necessity because it was easy to fall asleep with this posture. Subsequently, it soon became fashionable to drink tea in various temples with all the monks joining in to plant, collect and process tea leaves. Famous teas are often made from celebrated temples.

This Zen ritual developed into the tea ceremony of Japan in the fifteenth century.

The monks gathered before the figure of Dharma and drank tea from a single bowl with the profound formality of a holy sacrament in Chinese Zen Buddhism.

In the world of the Chinese Tao of Tea float the ripples of Zenist philosophy. These philosophies are unwritten, passed on by the soul, and grasped by the self in an instant. A well-known anecdote about "Zhaozhou Tea" is about Cong Shen, an established monk in the Tang dynasty, who used to be the abbot of Zhaozhou Temple. Many people came to this temple to ask for advice. One day, Master Cong Shen asked a monk, "Have

METAL

you been to our temple before?" "Yes," the monk admitted. "Go and drink the tea!" Cong Shen instructed. Then he turned to another monk and asked the same question. "Never," replied the monk. The master said, "Go and drink the tea!" The head of the temple was bewildered. "Master, why did you tell both of them to go and drink the tea, whether or not they had been here before?" he said. Cong Shen called his name. "Yes," the head of the temple responded. Once again, Cong Shen uttered, "Go and drink the tea!"

Why did he always instruct others to drink the tea? I think that he had something called *jifeng* beyond the words. *Jifeng*, the riddle-like answer of Zen, was attributed to the sixth Chinese patriarch Huineng (638-713) who was the founder of Southern Zen. A story about him began with two monks arguing why the flag of a pagoda flutters. One monk suggested that the wind moved it, while the other insisted that the flag moved itself. Huineng, who had observed the conversation, told them that neither the wind nor the flag moved, but something of their minds moved it. Connecting the former story of drinking tea with the latter one, we may explain them like this: On the same topic, different people have distinct opinions due to their various backgrounds. For instance, how to interpret the subjects of a win and defeat depends on your awakening. Tea could help to keep a clear head, according to Zen teachings.

WOOD

The forest in Yunnan Province in which the wild legendary tea trees were found still alive.

CHAPTER TWO
WOOD

1. Tea Categories

As an old saying goes, "Tea names are too many to remember, even for a life-long tea drinker." China has the largest variety of teas among all countries with over hundreds of superb kinds with worldly fame. What are the top 10? I believe the answer is subjective like *People* magazine's 50 "Most Beautiful People."

Through several thousand years, the varieties and processing methods of Chinese tea have undergone tremendous change from one dynasty to another. The use of some splendid ancient teas declines or even becomes extinct as new teas emerge in every era. Each new tea excels the last one, similar to how the waves that are behind in the Yangtze River drive on those in front. Every variety of tea has its own rise and fall in history.

First, we should know that the same fresh green leaves, as raw material, will turn into totally different processed tea. Modern tea can be divided into six major categories due to the diverse processing methods, as in the following chart. The 7th category is scented tea. It is a unique variety of tea, which doesn't belong to any of the six major tea categories. It has a re-processing process, during which, ready-made green tea, black tea, Oolong of the six major teas will be blended with fresh flowers. The tea leaves will slowly absorb the scent of the flowers in stillness. After a while, the farmers screen out the flower residue and dry the leaves, and the scented tea

Modern Chinese Tea	Categories	Features	Typical Types	Remarks
Six Tea Categories	Green Tea	Non-fermented	*①Xihu Longjing、*②Bi Luo Chun、*③Huangshan Maofeng、Pingshui Zhucha (pearl-shaped tea)、Taipin Houkui、Lushan Yunwu、Tunlu、Guzhu Zisun (Purple Bamboo Shoot)、Xinyang Maojian	Chinese green teas have the richest choices.
	Black Tea	Fully Fermented	*④Qimen Black Tea (Keemun)、Yunnan Black Tea 、Zhengshan Xiaozhong	
	Yellow Tea	Stacked	*⑤Junshan Yinzhen、Mengding Huangya (Yellow Bud)	
	White Tea	Steamed	*⑥Baihao Yinzhen、White Peony、Shoumei	
	Oolong Tea	Semi-fermented	*⑦Anxi Tie Guan Yin (Tieh Kwan Yin)、Huang Jingui	Grow in South Fujian
			*⑧Da Hong Pao (Red Robe)、TieLuohan、Bai Jiguan、Shui Jingui、Shuixian、Rougui	Grow in North Fujian
			*⑾Fenghuang Dancong	Grow in Guangdong
			*⑿Baihao Oolong、Dongding Oolong	Grow in Taiwan
	Dark Tea	Compressed	*⑨Pu'er Tea	Special definition
			Other Tea Bricks and Bowl Tea	
Reprocessing Tea	Scented Tea	Flower-scented	*⑩Jasmine Tea、Rose Tea	Scented
			*Red Point、Seven Fairladies	Artistic tea

* Highlighted in future chapters

will be obtained.

Green Tea: The majority of the famous teas in China are green teas. They contain more nutrients and chlorophyll compared with other teas due to the absence of fermentation during processing. Based on the production method, green teas include the fired ones such as Longjing and Bi Luo Chun, and steamed ones were popular in China before the Ming dynasty, nowadays there is Yulu of Japan that have a fresh jade-green color.

Yellow Tea: The production is similar to that of green tea, however, it is stacked so that its liquor appears yellow. Famous kinds are Junshan Yinzhen and Mengding Yellow Bud.

White Tea: It is steamed to retain its taste and scent of sunshine. Typical types are Baihao Yinzhen, Shoumei, and White Peony.

Oolong Tea: This unique Chinese tea variety, also known as semi-fermented, possesses distinctive characteristics, featured by both the fermentation of black tea and non-fermentation of green tea. The tea leaves are red at edge and green in the center after brewing. The varieties of Oolong include Tie Guan Yin tea, Wuyi rock tea and Taiwan Oolong.

Black Tea: This type is actually called red tea in Chinese. Full-fermention causes the red liquor in the cup. The popular ones are Qimen black tea, Yunnan black tea and Zhengshan Xiaozhong.

Dark Tea: These leaves are compressed into shapes of bricks, cakes, and bowls, for long-distance transpor-

Process of producing Longjing tea

The most popular tea species are distributed separately, especially in East, South and Southwest China.

tation and storage. Some teas in this category are Pu'er tea, Liubao tea and Hunan dark tea.

Now, let's learn more about some of the most popular Chinese teas today. They are the representatives of the 6 tea types mentioned above, most of which have unarguably led the list of the Top 10 teas for a very long time. Available at Chinese tea shops, these teas, full of pride and joy, wait for tea lovers to bring them home to enjoy.

2. Most Popular Chinese Teas

The most popular tea species are distributed separately, especially in East, South and Southwest China.

Xihu Longjing

Xihu Longjing tea has long been in first place among the Chinese teas. The tea gets its name, Longjing which means Dragon Well in Chinese, from the saying that a dragon once drank from a well there.

Crowned as "the queen of green tea", she was born in Hangzhou City, Zhejiang Province in East China. This city, called "heaven on earth", gets its fame from its beautiful West Lake (Xihu). The area producing Xihu Longjing tea is not far from West Lake. It is surrounded by mountains on three sides, which forms a natural barrier for a unique microclimate. Historically, five spots in this area produced the best Xihu Longjing tea. Now the finest ones are mainly from three spots, Shifeng Mountain, Meijia Wu and Xihu Longjing Village. Among the three, Shifeng (Lion Mount) Longjing is considered the

The map of Longjing tea area from the Qing dynasty

West Lake (Xihu)

The portrait of Emperor Qianlong

highest quality.

Longjing tea is famous for its jade-green color, delicate aroma, mellow taste and beauty of shape. Its appearance is characterized by smoothness, flatness, and straightness. Longjing tea is best when the leaves are fresh buds.

Have you heard of the term called "*Mingqian* Tea"?

Xihu Longjing

It means that farmers pick the tea before the Qingming Festival, which takes place in the 5th solar term of April. Known for its superior quality, *Mingqian* tea has tender buds and a rich fragrant smell. Unfortunately, *Mingqian* tea is especially rare. This means pre-Qingming Xihu Longjing tea is as expensive as fresh seafood such as fine Australian lobster or South African oysters, with the price changing everyday! *Mingqian* Shifeng Longjing's color isn't a common green like many would expect. The leaves contain some natural yellowish notes like that of brown rice.

Emperor Qianlong of the Qing dynasty, one of the most successful emperors in Chinese history, paid many visits to the Xihu Longjing Tea Area in Hangzhou during his tours to South China to show his concern for the folk people, according to legend. During a springtime visit, Emperor Qianlong saw a few village maids picking leaves from the tea bushes in front of the Hu Gong Temple where the birds sang delightfully in the air. Touched by the joyful scene, Qianlong couldn't help but to join the maids in picking the leaves. Suddenly a eunuch came to report that, the empress dowager (his mother) had fallen ill and wanted him to return immediately. Being a loving and respectful son, Emperor Qianlong dropped the tea leaves in his pocket and immediately returned to the Forbidden City without taking any breaks on the road. Whereas, in fact, the empress dowager's condition was not serious. She only had red and swollen eyes and some stomach discomfort. The delicate fragrance of the tea followed emperor when he rushed to see his mother. The empress dowager asked what he had brought after smelling the leaves.

At first, the Emperor did not realize where the smell came from until he touched his pocket with the leaves inside. It was the tea leaves from Shifeng Mountain of Hangzhou City. The empress dowager then asked to taste the tea. The maid of honor brewed the tea. The empress dowager felt much better after drinking the tea. With more drinks, her eyes and stomach all recovered. She happily commented, "It's really a panacea!" Seeing his mother so delighted, Emperor Qianlong immediately issued a decree, conferring the 18 tea bushes at the foot of Shifeng Mountain special imperial status. As a result, every year new Xihu Longjing tea leaves should be picked before the Qingming Festival and sent to the court as an imperial tribute.

Bi Luo Chun (Pi Lo Chun)

This tea is produced in Dongting Mountain in Wu County of Suzhou City, Jiangsu Province of East China. Another heavenly place like Hangzhou, Suzhou is the place where Xi Shi (during Spring and Autumn period), one of the most beautiful ladies in Chinese history, often spent her holidays 2500 years ago. Tea gardens and orchards grow here in the neighborhoods, bringing a special floral aroma and fruity taste to Bi Luo Chun.

Both considered supreme green teas, Bi Luo Chun and Xihu Longjing tea are easy to distinguish from each other because of their different processing techniques. Xihu Longjing is pressed flat, while Bi Luo Chun is rolled into a tight spiral and has a dark green color with snowy white hairs.

Seldom are tea names intriguing like that of Bi Luo Chun. Its name comes from a legend from the Qing dynasty. One day a tea picker ran out of space in her basket and placed the fresh tea leaves between her breasts. The tea, warmed by her body heat, emitted a strong aroma which caused

Suzhou garden in spring

other tea pickers to cry, "Xia Sha Ren Xiang" (Wuzhong dialect, meaning "scarily fragrant"). Emperor Kangxi (1654-1722), the grandfather of Emperor Qianlong, later visited Taihu Lake during his inspection tour. He greatly admired the tea after drinking it, but felt the name "Xia Sha Ren Xiang" was inelegant. The emperor gave it a more civilized name based on its features, "Bi Luo Chun." *Bi* refers to the color, *Luo* the shape and *Chun*

Incised windows of East China and Bi Luo Chun tea both feature delicacy. Collection of Guanfu Classic Art Museum.

Bi Luo Chun

the season it is harvested. Since then, the story of Bi Luo Chun became a tidbit among the annual tea tributes.

Collected in beauty's breasts and named by the emperor, how can an advertisement be more effective than this? The most precious Bi Luo Chun tea is the pre-Qingming, cropped and processed from Spring Equinox to Qingming Festival.

Huangshan Maofeng

Huangshan Maofeng, the most well-known Alpine green tea in China, originates from Anhui Province. It grows in the highest mountain in the eastern part of the country unlike Xihu Longjing and Bi Luo Chun. Huangshan Mountain is deemed the most famous Chinese mountain for its four wonders: strangely-shaped pines, grotesque rock formations, seas of clouds and hot springs. The environment is suited for the growth of tea with its high elevation, fine soil texture, and a warm and humid climate. It is "foggy everywhere from morning until night on a fine day, while cloudy when it's gloomy or rainy."

Huangshan Mountain

Top class Huangshan Maofeng has looks like gold pieces with ivory hair. The tea soap appears clear, and the light yellow tea leaves look like flowers in it.

A typical tea firm of Huizhou of the Qing dynasty

Huangshan Maofeng

Qimen Black Tea (Keemun or Qihong)

While it appears that black tea comes from red leaves, the full fermentation process causes the green leaves to turn a dark color.

Qimen black tea comes from the southwestern part of Anhui Province, near the production area of Huangshan Maofeng. The area that grows Qimen black tea has an advantageous natural condition: a great number of woods in a mountainous region, a warm and humid climate, and thick layers of earth with abundant rainfall, and cloudy or foggy weather most days of the year.

The Huizhou houses

The rich contents and high enzymatic activity in the soil make the local tea trees suitable for creating black tea. During the first year in the reign of Emperor Guangxu (in the year 1875), an Anhuinese resident and merchant, who admired the popularity of Fujian black tea, made the first successful batch of Qimen black tea.

Regarded as the champion among all teas in Britain, Qimen black tea was favored by the royal family and nobility. People would scramble every time fresh Qimen black tea came to a market. They believed that they "found the fragrance of spring in the aroma of the Chinese tea."

The Chinese began drinking black tea in the Southern Song dynasty over one thousand years ago. The Chinese prefer to drink black tea plain while the British prefer to drink it with milk and sugar along with some cakes as

Qimen Black Tea

breakfast tea or afternoon tea. Black tea shines even more brilliantly in the company of Wedgwood or Royal Albert drinkware. The tea's taste remains strong after milk is added. Thereafter, two styles of drinking black tea are formed. We can say that black tea originated in

Catherine of Braganza (1638-1705) was England's first tea drinking Queen. The English poet Edmund Waller (1606-1687) praised both the Queen and tea when he wrote the first eulogy of tea in English verse to honor the birthday of Queen Catherine in the year of her marriage to Charles II in 1662. The poem begins: Venus her myrtle, Phoebus has his bays; Tea both excels, which she vouch safes to praise.

The tea was exported from Shanghai port in the late Qing dynasty.

China, and further developed in Britain into the practice of afternoon tea. There is a story that when Sir Thomas Lipton, the holder of Yellow Label instant teabag, visited Shanghai, a rich Chinese person entertained him in his home. He expected to be a traditional Chinese tea when he asked for a cup, but was surprisingly served Lipton's tea with milk and sugar.

Anxi Tie Guan Yin (Tieh Kwan Yin)

Tie Guan Yin, the most typical Oolong tea, grows in Anxi County in the south of Fujian Province. The tea trees are planted in curved lines on the southeast slope of the mountain. From the sky, it looks like a carefully designed green labyrinth. During the late Qing dynasty, Anxi Tie Guan Yin (Tieh Kwan Yin) was successively introduced to Taiwan Province, and Guangdong Province, which promoted the development of Oolong tea there.

Black tea

How do you recognize Tie Guan Yin from other teas? Granular Tie Guan Yin weighs more than others in the same volume. It's rolled in balls before steeped in water. When fully infused, green tea leaves with red rims can clearly be seen. It differs from other Oolong teas for its natural orchid aroma and special appeal called

Anxi Tie Guan Yin

Guan Yin (Kwan-yin) is the Goddess of Mercy. Her female image in China is featured by kindness and clemency. For this reason, she is highly valued by the Chinese Buddhists in China and common people often pray to her for good luck.

"Guan Yin Yun" (mainly referring to its strong perfume, bursting flavor and lingering aftertaste).

The tea has a special name because it was a bestowment from Guan Yin (the Bodhisattva of Mercy) and named by the Emperor, according to the legends. In the Qing dynasty, there was an old farmer named Wei Yin who believed in Guan Yin. For many years, he piously worshiped Guan Yin every morning with a cup of tea. One night, he dreamt that he carried a hoe to a moun-

Women of the late Qing dynasty were selecting fine Oolong tea leaves.
This method is also preserved in the modern production of Tie Guan Yin tea.

tain stream nearby where he found a tea tree flourishing with lush leaves. The next morning, he went along the path in his dream, to really find a tea tree that looked exactly like the one from his dream. Another story says that after drinking the tea, Emperor Qianlong proclaimed, "Coming from the dream sent by Guan Yin and weighing like iron, this tea should have a more refined name like 'Iron Guan Yin'! (*tie*, in Chinese, means 'Iron')"

Da Hong Pao (Scarlet Robe or Red Robe)

Wuyi rock tea, a famous kind of Oolong in China, grows on the Wuyi Mountain of Fujian Province. The tea Da Hong Pao is outstanding among the rock teas. The tea trees come from Tianxin Yan Rock, but large tea gardens are not to be found here. There are only four tea trees growing at a sunken spot on the cliff called "Jiulong Ke" (literally meaning "Nine Dragon Cave"). In the sunshine, the tea shoots glistens with a lovely lustre of reddish purple.

Despite its black and loose look, Da Hong Pao actually has great brewing durability. Even after seven or eight infusions to keep the tea hot, its floral fragrance can still remain as if it penetrated the cover of the cup in an undispersed "cluster." The Da Hong Pao leaves can keep the "cluster" of aroma for a fairly long time at the

"Zhuangyuan" often refers to the candidate who won first place in the Civil Examinations. He would return home with a red robe after acquiring such a supreme honor. Da Hong Pao is also renowned as "'Zhuangyuan' amongst all teas" for its rarity.

Da Hong Pao

bottom of the cup, which is called "bottom fragrance" or "cold fragrance" by tea masters.

What does "Da Hong Pao" mean to the Chinese? First, it is not a common dress that anyone can put on. So Da Hong Pao in Chinese means sweetness begins when bitterness is finished. As a legend goes, a young student went to the capital to take the imperial examination at court level for the third time. He lived in an inn where he had three dreams one night before the exam. In the first dream, he dreamt of himself planting cabbages on the wall; in the second, he was wearing a bamboo hat while holding an umbrella on a rainy day; the third, he was sleeping with his beloved girl back to back. The next day, the student hurried to find a fortune-teller to interpret the meaning behind the dreams.

Wuyi Mountain

After hearing the dreams, the fortune-teller shook his head, "It's too bad. You'd better go home. Think about it. What can you get planting cabbages on a wall? Nothing! What's the use of a bamboo hat if you are holding an umbrella? Unnecessary! And sleeping back to back with your lover? Completely hopeless!" The student went back to the inn to pack his belongings in despair.

The inn keeper was surprised, "Aren't you taking the exam tomorrow? Why are you leaving today?" The student told him about the fortune-teller. The inn keeper was amused, "I can interpret dreams, too. On the contrary, I think you should stay. Think about it again. Planting on a high wall, doesn't it mean that you'll pass the exam with a high score (the Chinese words for 'plant' and 'pass' are homophones)? Wearing a bamboo hat while holding an umbrella, doesn't it mean you'll be safe in the exam because of your preparation? Lying back to back on the bed, doesn't it mean that it's your turn to change the position now because you've worked hard for so many years?" These words convinced the student to stay. He went to the exam cheerfully and won "Zhuangyuan" (the first place). He was finally able to wear the red robe (Da Hong Pao).

In the past, when the tea trees shot up, monks of Tianxin Temple would gather the monkeys they tamed with drums. The monkeys, dressed in red, would climb up the cliff to pick tea leaves. Nowadays, tea farmers in Mount Wuyi will set up high aerial ladders instead of using monkeys. The total output of rock tea is limited because they can normally only pick about 11 *liang* (a unit of weight equal to 50 grams). The tea can now be produced and put into the market in batches with clone technology.

The monkeys picking and gathering tea is an early and fanciful legend in China. This is an illustration from an old book.

Dongting Lake

Junshan Yinzhen (Jun Mountain Silver Needle)

Junshan Yinzhen is produced in Junshan Island at the center of Dongting Lake in Hunan Province, the second largest fresh water lake of China. The lake has long been praised by major poets like Li Bai. Four thousand years ago, Emperor Shun died during his inspection tour in this area, according to legends. His two beloved concubines hastened to an island for his funeral. After their arrival, the concubines watched the boundless Dongting Lake with tears running down their faces. The island Junshan literally means "Imperial Mountain."

Junshan Yinzhen is a yellow tea that resembles the shape of a needle. Mainly composed by bud teas, it is called "gold inlaid with jade" for its plump yet compact look with a golden shine and tiny white hairs. More attention has been paid to its appreciation value than other teas. It is a feast for the eyes to watch the infusion of Junshan Yinzhen through a transparent glass. In the hot water, the tea buds stand upright like silver needles, then sink gradually to the bottom, and rise up again slowly like the dancing concubines of Emperor Shun. This process repeats itself for three rises and falls. This is one of the most prominent features of Junshan Yinzhen.

When wiping their tears, the concubines' hands tinctured the bamboos they were holding with speckles of tears. The bamboos were later named Xiangfei Bamboo (Xiangfei refers to the two concubine of Emperor Shun).

Junshan Yinzhen

Baihao Yinzhen (White Hair Silver Needle)

Baihao Yinzhen, the supreme variety of white tea, comes from Fujian Province, a place known for producing the imperial tribute tea during the Song dynasty. As

Shoumei refers to the long white eyebrows of an old person.

Song people believed for tea, "The whiter, the more precious." Some modern experts claim that white tea existed for a thousand years, and, merchants have asked for exorbitant prices using this so-called "evidence." Personally I think it's an interpretation without real understanding which can easily mislead consumers. In the second chapter of the book, I mentioned that Emperor Huizong of the Song dynasty highly recommended black rabbit's hair-patterned cup for a better appreciation of the white tea foam not today's fermented white teas that came from the Ming and Qing dynasties.

Baihao Yinzhen is made from single fresh buds, approximately 3 cm long, from newborn tea trees in the spring. Covered all over with white hairs, its color is neither verdant like green tea, crimson as black tea, nor as brown as Oolong tea. It is called "silver needle" for its lustre of silver green.

Baihao Yinzhen

Scenery in Fujian Province

Shangri-La is the important town on the ancient "Tea-Horse Road" to Tibet.
This route played a historical role in the solidarity and trades between the Han and Tibetan.

Pu'er Tea

"Cropped by grandfather, enjoyed by grandson," the process of Pu'er tea takes several decades from its harvest to drinking.

Pu'er, a kind of dark tea, comes from Yunnan Province where there are many subtropical forests. It is associated in a folk legend with Zhuge Liang (styled Kongming, 181-234), who was the most intelligent Chinese figure during the Three Kingdoms period.

At that time, Yunnan was under the control of Meng Huo, a local warlord. He was caught by Zhuge Liang in a battle. Zhuge brought Meng to look around the Shu military camps and asked, "How about my troops?"

"Well, I lost because I did not know your actual situation. Thank you for letting me see the condition of Shu's army. I could win if there were another battle," said Meng.

Zhuge laughed and set Meng free against the advice of all of his subordinates. Zhuge told his generals that people will only be loyal when you outperform them with morals and merits, not with your power. Meng was captured and set free total seven times before he finally accepted his failure, and promised loyality to the Shu Kingdom. Zhuge let Meng still keep his army and left no Shu troops in Yunnan after helping them to set up the legal system. In this case, the best way to win a battle is to destroy the enemy's determination to fight, rather than directly attacking the walled city. It's the conclusions in Sun-tzi's *The Art of War*.

Pu'er tea

Episodes from *The Romance of Three Kingdoms*, collection from China Guanfu Classic Art Museum

During this battle, many soldiers suffered eye diseases because of climate sickness and could not fight. To cure the soldiers, Zhuge Liang took out a walking stick and plugged it into the rock of Nannuo Mountain in Xishuangbanna in Yunnan. The stick instantly turned into a green tea tree. The soldiers all recovered after drinking the tea. In this way, the first tea tree was born, and six tea mountains producing Pu'er tea formed around it.

Different from other tea leaves, Pu'er tea is made from big-leaf tea tree in various shapes of "cakes." It is a type of dark tea which mainly uses coarse and old raw materials. Its tea soup distinguishes itself from other teas from its red wine-like look, soft and smooth taste as well as an aged aroma unique to itself.

In conclusion, Pu'er tea's quality improves the longer it's preserved, because of its purer taste. It is the only tea that is valued by its age. Some aged Pu'er tea in the tea stock of the Forbidden City has existed for a hundred years. It has now become a hot spot for collection and investment as a "drinkable antique."

Various flowers for scenting teas

Scented Tea (Flower-scented Tea)

Scented tea is mainly from Fujian, Zhejiang, Anhui and Jiangsu Province, because these places also produce fresh flowers. Scented tea is named after the flowers used in its production. Some popular varieties include, jasmine tea, rose tea and osmanthus tea.

Scented tea is a unique variety of tea, which doesn't belong to any of the six major tea categories. It is made through a reprocessing process where ready-made teas from the six major teas are blended with fresh flowers. The tea leaves are left for a while to slowly absorb the scent of the flowers. The final step in the process involves the farmers screening out the flower residue and drying the leaves.

Being Beijing-born, I know quite well that scented tea, also called *xiang pian* (silvers of perfume), is extremely popular in Northern China. A method of blending valuable

Scented tea

perfume into supreme green tea already existed as early as 1000 years ago in the Song dynasty. One typical flower used to scent tea is jasmine. Chinese people love jasmine so much that there is a famous folk song about it. The melody was adopted by Puccini in his opera *Turandot*.

You can see an example of scented tea in the recent film *Marie Antoinette* directed by Sofia Coppola. When the French Queen played by Kirsten Dunst, invites her brother to look at a mysterious treasure from faraway Orient. She says, "The Emperor of China sent me this tea. Watch the flower (water pouring…). Isn't it divine?" While the two stare at the cup , a white fog rises from the exquisite china cup and they are surprised to see a red flower blossom slowly from a bunch of green tea. The queen proudly tells her brother that it's jasmine tea. This magic tea used by Marie Antoinette to show off her luxurious royal life is actually a kind of Chinese artistic tea. It hides the flowers in a tea ball bound by green tea leaves and expands when infused with boiling water. I don't mind seeing this very modern artistic flower tea in a film that took place two centuries ago. Rather, I'd be quite pleased.

Rose tea

Sofia Coppola let Marie Antoinette (by Kirsten Dunst) show Chinese artistic tea in the film.

EARTH

There are corresponding utensils for each particular tea types.

CHAPTER THREE

EARTH

Even with a fine tea in hand, the right choice of tea utensils is still crucial for making a nice cup of tea. An ancient saying goes "The utensil is the father of tea," and the correct use of it will reveal not only its scientific function, but also the aesthetic appreciation of the drinker. First of all, you would not use a red wine glass to appreciate the bubbles called the "splendid stars of champagne." Secondly, the choice of the wide-brimmed champagne saucer or tall, thin champagne tulip depends on the occasion, visual effect or just drinker's personal preference. If you can understand this, then you will understand the requirements on choosing Chinese teawares.

Why is the knowledge of tea utensils more complex than that of wine glasses? Using the wrong utensils can result in wasting the precious tea. For instance, someone who uses glass cup and warm water to brew Tie Guan Yin could find the tea "tasteless with a lot of stalks and old leaves." Similarly, Longjing tea can taste bitter and astringent if infused with boiling water in a large porcelain kettle, and covered it for a long time before pouring it out. We will miss the joy in tea drinking if we make such mistakes.

Generally, we need to consider three factors when choosing tea utensils: the location, the number of drinkers, and the species of tea leaves. There are corresponding utensils for each particular tea types. For example, a superb green tea should be matched with colorless transparent glass without any ornamentation. Oolong tea should be steeped in refined *Zisha* (purple clay) teapots, scented tea in bowls with a cover to retain its aroma, and ordinary green tea in large porcelain teapots.

1. The ABCs of Tea Sets

1-2. Boiling kettle with a stove

3. *Gaiwan*—China's classic tea set. The claim that *gaiwan* is used informally with friends is wrong. In fact, I found that *gaiwan* was served even in royal banquets.

4. (Left) Cup for sniffing scent (Right) Little tea cup

6. Tea bowl (with a high-heel saucer)

7. Small dish for appreciating dry tea

5. Tea pot

8. Tea caddy

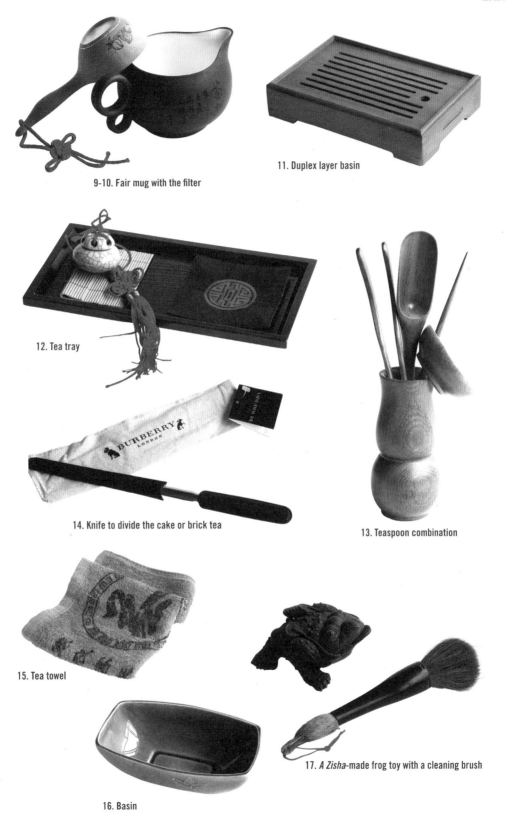

9-10. Fair mug with the filter

11. Duplex layer basin

12. Tea tray

13. Teaspoon combination

14. Knife to divide the cake or brick tea

15. Tea towel

16. Basin

17. *A Zisha*-made frog toy with a cleaning brush

2. Features of *Zisha* Teapots

A Chinese tea addict usually holds a small teapot in hand for both infusing and drinking alone. It is known as the Yixing *Zisha* teapot, which appeared in the early Northern Song dynasty, and gained momentum in the Ming dynasty. "The clay in the teapot is worth even more than gold," according to a local saying.

Zisha teapots are very popular despite their high prices due to their advantages for tea drinkers.

Zisha pots can maintain freshness of the tea for long periods of time. A

Zisha tea set

Yixing cabinet-style *Zisha* teapot after the Qing dynasty

legend says that a carpenter forgot a half-full *Zisha* teapot on a crossbeam near the rooftop while renovating a house. Years later he found the teapot when he came to work on the same house again. To his surprise, the tea in the teapot still retained a faint scent instead of turning sour.

They can also help bring out the tea's flavor. Long ago there was a rich man who was also a tea lover. One day, a beggar came to him, "Mister, I heard that you are very knowledgable about tea, could you kindly offer me some?"

The rich man gave him a cup of tea. "The tea is fine, but the flavor is not rich enough, because you're using a new teapot," said the beggar, after drinking the tea. He then brought out an age-old teapot.

The rich man looked at the teapot. It was really a fantastic one. The beg-

Eighteen shapes of *Zisha* teapots designed by Chen Mansheng of the Qing dynasty

gar opened the lid to pour in clear water. Without any tea leaves, the pot itself immediately emitted a delicate fragrance.

The rich man wanted to buy it, but the beggar said, "This teapot was passed down from my ancestors. I can't entirely sell it to you. It's worth 3000 *liang* (a unit of weight equal to 50 grams) of gold. Now I can sell half of it to you, if you give me 1500 *liang* of gold so I can settle down my family, and I'll come here often to use it together with you. How's that?"

The rich man readily agreed, and the beggar kept his promise. He often came by to drink tea with the rich man like they were old friends.

The teapot has great artistry along with its ability to improve the taste of tea. A Yixing local legend says that, "The artistry (of *Zisha* teapot) was created by the monks in Jinsha Temple, while accomplished by Gong Chun." Gong Chun was a poor boy attendant during the Ming dynasty, who served his master during his study. When the boy was free, he would often play in a small temple nearby called "Jinsha Temple" and help the old monks there do some trifles. The old monks earned their living through pottery. Later, Gong Chun wanted to learn the artistry of pottery making from them, but the monks rejected him because they were afraid that they may lose their job by teaching others. Gong Chun decided to learn the craft by secretly watching the monks make teapots. Later, he added in his own improvements. He first made green ware from fine panned clay by pressing the inner wall with a spoon, and the outer wall with his fingers. He would keep pressing it until the final pot was made with his finger prints remaining on its belly. Gong Chun's works combined simplicity and elegance. It was a breakthrough compared with the previous *Zisha* teapots. (I have consulted ancient books, and feel that

A Gong Chun teapot

this might be the reason why the Forbidden City did not accept the *Zisha* teapot into its collection until the early Qing dynasty.) It successfully promoted Yixing tea pottery into an artistic form, which was well received by the royalty and the general public. Generations later, potters even worked together with scholars in making new irresistibly beautiful pot styles like creating fashion designs. Looking at the various fantastic masterpieces of *Zisha* teapot, I couldn't help wondering, what would it be if John Galliano from Christian Dior were invited to design a fabulous *Zisha* teapot?

Lastly, these teapots command a high price due to the rarity of its raw material. In the whole world, *Zisha* clay (purple clay) is said to only exist in the Yellow Dragon Cave of Dingshan town in Yixing. It only takes up 3 percent of the entire clay there. Some have even made a fortune by simply buying up the market of *Zisha* clay. When Gong Chun found that he could not afford the clay, he suddenly remembered the sink where the old monks washed their hands everyday. He then hurried to the sink to find a thick layer of *Zisha* sediment when he reached his hands to the bottom . Overjoyed by his discovery, Gong Chun immediately began ladling it out with a wooden scoop and screening out the clay with great patience. He eventually finished his first masterpiece this way.

How can I find a good *Zisha* teapot?

i. In an overview, the spout, mouth and handle of the teapot should all touch the surface of the table if turned upside down.

ii. The water pours out smoothly without leaks. When the tea is served, the water at the mouth of the teapot should immediately fall back to the belly, without dripping out of the mouth of the tea pot.

iii. Fill up the teapot with water and cover it with the lid.

Block up the pot mouth and turn the pot upside down. It's a good pot if the lid doesn't fall,

Then keep the pot upside down, hold the lid while unblocking the mouth. It's also a sign of a good pot if the water doesn't come out.

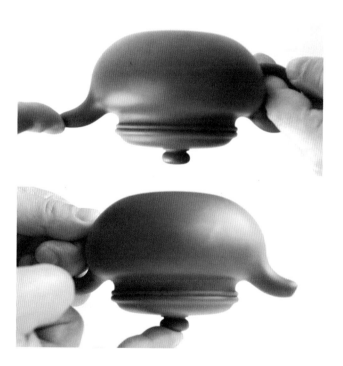

Now that we've picked up a fine teapot, we need to be careful in its maintenance:

1. After you buy a teapot, cleanse it with water before boiling it in a large kettle of strong tea. After it cools off, boil it again. Repeat the whole process for three times, pick it up and dry it by airing. The teapot is now usable for tea making.

2. When making tea, pour hot water in the pot and around it for several rounds, and then wipe the body of the teapot with wet towel or clean wet cloth for a while.

3. After the temperature of the pot body goes down, you can also rub it with your own hands. The oil and sweat from your hands can help keep the pot body shiny and smooth. Keep doing it for three or four months, the teapot will have a better appearance.

4. Avoid getting greasy stains from food on the tea-pot.

3. Features of Porcelain Tea Utensils

Between the two major types of Chinese tea utensils, *Zisha* and ceramics, porcelain sets came much earlier and have been a part of the entire historical evolution of the Chinese tea.

A blue glazed porcelain tea bowl with a saucer (Southern dynasties)

The clay-made cooker with caddy and pot in it (Original porcelain, Han dynasty)

Why are the porcelain tea utensils so dazzlingly distinct from the Tang, the Song and the Ming dynasties?

The reason is that the methods of tea drinking were different from one dynasty to the next. From brewing cake tea in the Tang dynasty, infusing powdered tea in the Song dynasty, to steeping leaf tea in the Ming dynasty, many ancient Chinese tea drinkers cared about not only the shape of the utensils in releasing the best taste of the tea soup, but also matching the color of the tea to evoke the highest sense of aesthetic beauty. The special interest of ancient Oriental people in tea sets reflected their pursuit of a high quality life.

The first mature form of blue glazed porcelain emerged in the Shangyu district of Zhejiang Province during the Eastern Han dynasty. The blue color porcelain produced by Yue Kiln represented of its popular kind in the states of Han and Jin. A poem written during the Han dynasty told a story of the poet himself on a spring outing with his friends on a mountain for a tea party with his Yue Kiln tea sets.

In the Tang dynasty, the blue glazed porcelain in the south and the white glazed in north China gradually earned equal shares in the market. Lu Yu had a famous conclusion on that, "The tea soup (at that time) is

White kettle with double gradin heads (Sui dynasty)

The Yue Kiln tea bowl (Tang dynasty)

Rabbit's hair-patterned cup from the Song dynasty, Jian Kiln

A tea bowl and saucer of Jun Kiln (Song dynasty)

Celadon tea bowl (Song dynasty)

slightly reddish, while the blue porcelain looks heavy in color with a touch of jade. When the two are matched together, they form a pleasing contrast in an elegant manner. Though Xingzhou porcelain shines in pure white and resembles silver, it won't be a good match for tea soup, for it's a bit too light in color." Lu Yu and others in the Tang dynasty considered blue glazed porcelain tea bowls as the best tea utensils.

This also helps us understand why the first choice of utensils for tea changed from blue porcelain to black one during the Song dynasty. The tea drinkers in those days usually whisked tea soups with a *chaxian* (tea whisk) to form pure white foams. Black was undoubtedly the best choice in order to contrast with the white foams and more importantly, to help the judge decide which tea owner won. The five kilns—Ru, Guan, Ge, Jun and Ding—were known for the unprecedented beauty of their products. The fineness of the porcelain texture, the pureness of the glaze, the creation of the shape had reached a higher level. The crackle on the glaze surface from Ge Kiln winded like an earthworm. The pleasing flambé glaze color of Jun Kiln resembled pink clouds or roses. The tea cups made by Longquan Kiln (Celadon) were shaped like upside-down bamboo hats and covered completely in a light cyan glaze.

In the Ming dynasty, people's choices over the color of tea utensils enormously changed again. When loose tea came to their table, drinkers mainly used white, blue and white or colored porcelain from Jingdezhen Kiln. These cups accentuated the freshness of the green soup for they were regarded "as thin as paper, as white as jade, as sonorous as chime stone and as bright as mirror."

Porcelain during the Qing dynasty under the reigns of Emperors Kangxi, Yongzheng and Qianlong were the best of its kind throughout the country. New varieties such as famille rose and enamel porcelain came into exis-

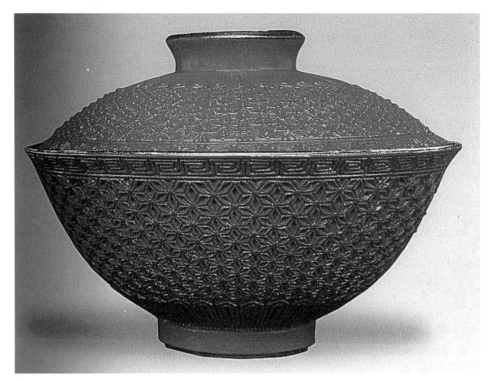

A coral red glazed *gaiwan* (Qing dynasty)

tence. Innovations in its decoration included various inscriptions, legends, pictures of famous scenic sites and lucky patterns.

Porcelain tea utensils contain a gold mine of cultural messages from where we can breathe the lush scent of history. The Chinese today can infer

Blue and white tea caddy covered with a lid (Jingdezhen Kiln, Ming dynasty)

Lu Jun glazed teapot (Yixing Kiln, Qing dynasty)

Blue and white tea cup (Jingdezhen Kiln, Ming dynasty)

The author's private collection: (Top) The 7501 ceramics specially produced for Chairman Mao Zedong has a shell as thin as that of an egg. (Bottom) Wenge porcelain tea tray

the time period in which it was fired from the picture and figures drawn on it. And it would also take people to tell whether such a set belonged to the 1950s or the 1960s because the porcelain utensils vividly captured the image of those years.

Enamel porcelain tea cup (Qing dynasty)

WATER

Chinese tea drinkers have always emphasized the water used in tea ceremonies.

Chapter Four

WATER

Chinese tea drinkers have always emphasized the water used in infusion. Through the water, a tea drinker takes in the pleasures of tea, including the fragrance, sweetness and purity of the crystal-clear tea liquor. Therefore, the choice of water is also a science. Only after the right water is prepared, we can enjoy the art of tea.

1. How to Choose the Right Water for Making Tea

Lu Yu was the first to discuss the relationship between tea and the quality of water. In *The Classic of Tea*, he ranked the quality of water used in tea brewing this way: "mountain water best, river water next, well water worst". He believed that mountain water (i.e. mountain spring) was the best to steep tea because its rich content of minerals were beneficial to the human body. Among mountain springs, the spring flowing slowly above the rocks was the best. By contrast, torrential mountain streams containing too many minerals were harmful to human beings. Stagnant ponds in complete stillness were not usable for tea infusion either because snake venom could have polluted it. Nor was stale water in a valley, which was often filled with deadwoods and withered leaves. If using river water, choose the one farthest from residences to avoid pollution. If unavoidable, choose a well frequented by other

A government official named Li Jiqing greatly admired the tea talent of Lu Yu, and invited Lu to have dinner together. During the dinner, he asked Lu to brew the tea with the famous "Nanling" water. Situated at the center of the Yangtze River, the mouth of the spring only emerges as the tide recedes. Thus, Li sent a servant to fetch a bottle of the water by boat. After the servant returned, Lu Yu scooped up some water and commented, "It's from the Yangtze River but not the Nanling Spring. It must be the water at the riverbank." Li glanced at the servant, who immediately vowed that, "I did fetch the right water. I have many witnesses." Lu Yu didn't reply. He poured out the water slowly and halted suddenly when half of the water was gone. Again he scooped up some water and said, "This part is indeed the water from the Nanling Spring." Amazed by this, the servant knelt down to confess, "I did fetch the Nanling water, but the boat swung violently on the way back and spilt out half of the water in the bottle. I was afraid that you might feel the quantity is too small so I filled up the rest of the bottle with the water at the riverside." Li and his guests were all astonished by Lu Yu's extraordinary connoisseurship of water.

people to ensure the freshness of the water.

Even though most tap water in modern cities reaches sanitation standards, it often contains calcium bicarbonate, magnesium bicarbonate, sulfate and chloride under ionization. Water with overly high contents of $Ca+$, $Mg2+$ and $Fe3+$ ions, called hard water, is unsuitable for tea infusion. When I lived at Peking University, I could always see there a black "oil" floating on the surface of boiled tea liquor, which indicated the tap water in Beijing was hard water. After flying to my Shanghai's studio, the black oil never appeared. So the soft tap water in East China or Southern China (i.e. Hong Kong) is more suited for tea.

With the right water, the timing of its boiling is still crucial. If overly boiled, the water will increase the content of the nitrate poisonous to humans and thus becomes undrinkable. In the same way, if the water is not

The soft tap water is more suited for tea.

boiled enough, the temperature will not be high enough to fully dissolve the beneficial substances in tea leaves. As a result, the fragrance and flavor of the tea won't be well presented.

In addition, different teas require various water temperatures for tea making. Generally speaking, the tender and delicate green tea should be steeped with water at around 85℃. Teas like Bi Luo Chun, *Mingqian* Longjing and Junshan Yinzhen shouldn't be infused with boiling water. It is preferable to steep Oolong and scented tea with boiled water at 95℃. For Oolong teas such as Da Hong Pao, black teas like Yunnan black tea, Qimen black tea, and Pu'er tea only infusing with boiling water can fully bring out their flavor. It's best to drink it right after it's been infused for 1 to 3 minutes by the water. To keep it fresh, do not infuse tea for more than five minutes.

Tibetan's favourite: Butter tea

People in Xinjiang traditionally drink tea with milk.

2. Tea Art and Ceremonies

Tea has its periods and different styles as art, which can be roughly classified into three stages: the Boiled Tea, the Whipped Tea, and the Steeped Tea. The Chinese ethnic minority groups have also formed their own unique tea customs.

We moderns belong to the Steeped Tea stage. If using a main tea set, the two infusion manners are through the teapot or cups. Infusing by teapot means brewing the tea leaves inside the pot first, take the Qimen black tea, Pu'er or Da Hong Pao as an example, and then pour the liquor into cups. Obviously, infusing by cups means directly using the cup, glass or cover-bowl cup (*gaiwan*) to brew and drink. The latter is suitable for superior Spring tea such as Bi Luo Chun, Huangshan Maofeng, Junshan Yinzhen or Xihu Longjing tea picked before the Pure Brightness Festival.

How to appreciate the Chinese tea ceremonies?

It is very important to bear in mind that Chinese tea art has its unique aesthetic style. From my point of view, its movements are like finger dancing with an opera-like plot. A graceful show of tea art is on when a tea sommelier slowly stretches out her wrists. While she fetches a tea utensil, you are seeing her fingers move like seeing the first blossom of a lotus flower. When she holds the cup and moves it, it's like an orchid floating in the air. While she pours the water, perhaps the kettle mouth is bobbing up and down like the nodding of a phoenix. While she turns the cup, its rim is displayed in full like a peacock spreading its tail. While she warms the cup, perhaps you are watching her fingers quickly roll the cup as if watching a traditional Chinese lion playing with a ball, or, while she pours out the last few drops of tea, it's like the general making his rounds, playing fair with every soldier of his troop without leaving anyone behind. The whole set of gestures are completed in a continuous gentle flow without any breaks, just like following the movements of Tai-Chi, where there seems to be a spirit floating and transferring in between, revealing the beauty and richness of its vitality.

Actually, a top master is a moving work of art during the tea ceremony. She gradually forms her own style that enriches her character, body language, and choreography to improve the performance. Next, you will see some pictures of the three main styles of Chinese tea art (photographs by Roy Le, staring Ling Yun). Normally the design of costumes, selection of tea sets and stage props as well as some unique processes of the tea ceremonies are presented according to the understanding and creativity of the tea master. So, you may also call the following ceremonies the "Ling Yun Style."

Longjing Tea Ceremony (using glass sets)

How to make a good cup of tea?

Let's take Longjing, the most famous Chinese tea, as an example. Personally I prefer *gaiwan*, but today's tea houses all use transparent glass. On the other hand, the glass is easy for us to watch the green leaves dance. Furthermore, the skill of using glass is relatively simple, allowing us to appreciate super-fine Longjing any place.

    1. Make a bow.

    2. Place the tools.

    3. Appreciate the Longjing tea.

    4. Appreciate the famous Hupao Spring water from Hangzhou City. Put a coin or other small flat things on it. If the coin can float, it shows the water, which has large surface tension, is suitable for making tea.

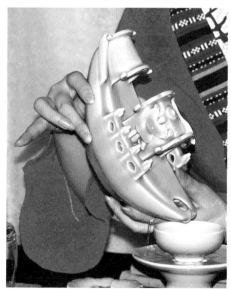

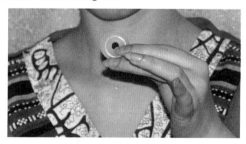

5. Warm the glass.

6. Put in tea.

Moisten.

Brew. Start with holding the kettle high to pour the water from above and then bring it closer to the glass. Repeat three times, like a phoenix nodding to express its appreciation to the guests.

7. Present the tea. The host must serve the tea respectfully using both hands to hold the glass, while saying softly "enjoy your tea." The guest, at the same time, should slightly move his body forward and express gratitude.

Enjoy drinking the tea.

Kung Fu Tea Art (using *Zisha* teapot)

Kung Fu tea art originated in Chaozhou-Shantou District of Guangdong Province in South China, with Kung Fu actually meaning "brewing tea with great skill." It came into being in the Qing dynasty, and still retains the most ancient drinking methods, especially with tea sets and infusion technique. For instance, the four treasures of Kung Fu tea utensils include a special clay stove with matching kettle, the Yixing small teapot and thin white porcelain cups. On the other hand, we usually use Fenghuang Dancong from the Mount Phoenix region in Chaozhou or Wuyi rock tea alternative.

1. Beginning gesture: add water to the kettle.

2. Fan the stove.

3. Water the teapot and cups.

4. Place the tea on a clean white paper to arrange the leaves according to their sizes. Then move the tea leaves into the pot.

5. Lift the kettle high to brew.

6. Remove the foam. Put the lid back and pour the hot water over surface of the teapot.

7. Lion rolling the ball: clean the tea cups skillfully and gracefully in the boiling water.

8. Distribute the tea like the Lord Guan (Guan Yu, 160-219, general in the period of Three Kingdoms) making an inspection of the city wall.

9. Pour the tea until the last drop into every teacup like the legendary General Han (?-196 BC, strategist in the Qin and Han dynasties) mustering the troops.

10. Presenting tea. When the host serves tea or adds water for his/her guests, some guests will knock the table rhythmically using bended middle finger and forefinger of their right hand to express their thanks.

Oriental Beauty's Tea Art (using porcelain sets)

Taiwan Oolong originated in Fujian and has formed its own characteristics. The Taiwanese also developed traditional tea art with their wisdom. Since we have watched an infusion with a small clay teapot, porcelain *gaiwan* will be used to carry on this demonstration.

1. Display the tea utensils.

2. Warm up the *gaiwan* and teacups.

3. Appreciate the tea.

4. Put in tea.

5. Initial soak.

6. Brew.

7. Move the foam.

8. Distribute the tea from the *gaiwan* with the thumb, index and middle fingers like three dragons escorting an ancient vessel.

9. Turn the cups upside down like a peacock spreading its tail to show its finest feathers.

10. Present the tea.

11. Enjoy the tea. | 12. Sip the tea.

FIRE

The selection of tea is an art.

CHAPTER FIVE

FIRE

It's not easy to select the right tea. In fact, it requires a fairly wide knowledge, including its classification and rating, pricing and market, evaluation and inspection methods. Choosing tea can be as professional as choosing diamonds.

In everyday life, we often have tea in storage for our own use or to entertain our guests. Therefore, the preservation of tea is also quite important.

1. The "Golden Rules" for Selecting Good Tea

When buying tea, we sometimes meet dishonest sellers falsifying supreme teas with common tea leaves in order to make staggering profits. A buyer needs to be more careful when buying more famous teas such as the ones introduced in the second chapter. The following "golden rules" can help you decipher whether a tea is of high quality or not.

Bi Luo Chun can be judged by its tenderness and hairiness.

Leaf shapes of well-known teas vary from strips, flat, needles, granule, to pearl-like, bricks, cakes, flakes and powder.

Observe the appearance of the tea leaves:

A. The features of well-known teas

Leaf shapes vary from strips, flat, needles, granule, to pearl-like, bricks, cakes, flakes and powder. Some varieties such as Bi Luo Chun can be judged by its tenderness and hairiness. A superior tea is more tender and hairy. Good tea leaves are nearly rid of all impurities like tea stalks, fragments, and withered pieces.

B. The color of tea

There are mainly six different colors of tea: red, green, yellow, white, black and cyan. If divided by tone, we have verdure, celadon, bottle green, dark green, and kelly. For example, the precious *Mingqian* Shifeng Longjing tea normally has a slight yellowish color. Although everyone seems to like

verdure "Longjing," it's a cheap counterfeit produced somewhere else instead of the real Xihu Longjing. This is a common mistake often made when choosing tea leaves.

C. The dryness of tea

High quality tea leaves usually have a low water content, which can be felt by touching them. The dryness of the leaf is ideal if it breaks easily with a slight pinch and your finger feels a light sting. Damp and soft leaves will produce a relatively poor taste and scent when steeped with water.

D. The aroma of tea

The buyer can smell the tea's aroma right after the tin is opened. He/She can also place some tea on the palm to see if there is a stale or peculiar smell.

Never rely entirely upon the recommendations of the shop owner. Try a cup of tea soup yourself:

A. The tea soup

No matter what type, a good cup of tea should be bright, fresh and clear. A cup of low quality tea is often dark and turbid.

B. Color of the tea soup

Qimen black tea, a popular tea in Britain, has a bright red. Oolong tea soup should be golden yellow, green tea soup yellowish green, and white tea a light apricot hue.

The bright red tea soup is essential for fine black tea.

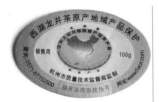

The mark of Xihu Longjing origin

C. The unfolding of tea leaves

Fresh leaves after fine processing will gradually unfold after several infusions. The tea soup is often rich in flavor with high brewing durability. If the tea leaves spread out too soon after the water is poured, they are probably old leaves with a plain taste and low brewing

Green leaves with red rims

durability.

D. Aroma after infusion

Good tea liquor should have a pure aroma, while terrible tea a faint, no aroma or even a peculiar smell. The smell of the leaves can show whether it was overheated, fully heated or under heated during its production processing.

E. Tea tasting

A tea can taste strong, fresh, sweet, tasty, mellow,

pure, mild, bitter or light. For instance, a good green tea tastes a little bitter with an aftertaste. Sweet black teas are superb ones, while those that taste astringent are inferior ones.

F. The aroma remaining at the bottom of the cup after the tea soup cools off

At this moment, the scent covered by the high tem-

perature has been revealed just like a perfume that has a top, middle, and base note.

G. The unfolded tea leaves after infusion

See if the tea leaves are tender, even, neat, and complete without impurities or burnt scars. All unfermented precious teas like Maojian tea, Maofeng tea and Silver Needle should have a large proportion of buds. When fully infused, the soft fleshy leaves of Tie Guan Yin spread out to show red rims and silky smooth surfaces.

Check the marks of origin or anti-fake labels, especially when buying rare teas such as Xihu Longjing, Anxi Tie Guan Yin (Tieh Kwan Yin) and Pu'er tea.

Teas for each season
Spring: Drinking scented tea in the spring can help emit the pathogenic cold stored up by the human body through winter, with its full aroma activating the generation of *yang qi* or energy.
Summer: Green tea is highly recommended in summer for its properties of bitterness and cold, which can help remove heat and toxic substances, quench thirst and strengthen the heart.
Autumn: During autumn it is better to drink Oolong tea. Neither too cold nor too hot, Oolong tea can refresh the body.
Winter: Black tea is an ideal winter drink. With a pleasant sweetness and temperateness, it contains rich protein to help digestion.

Have the tea packaged on site to avoid the seller from replacing the good tea with a bad tea after sampling.

In the end, the high prices do not often mean good quality. It might be a fake label or selling low quality tea at a very high price unless it is recognized by a trustworthy and honest tea expert.

In summary, I should emphasize that your own preference of taste is very important, even if the tea that you like is not the major promotion item of the shop. Trust yourself. This is also applicable to the selection of your cup of tea.

2. How to Store Tea?

After the tea is selected, we need to know how to preserve it. Tea leaves can easily absorb moisture and peculiar smells. High temperature or humidity, exposure to the sunlight or sufficient oxygen can cause a change in its content or even reduce the quality within a fairly short amount of time.

The way of storing supreme green tea

1. Supreme green tea, yellow tea and white tea: Among all the teas, they are the easiest to decay, become stale and lose color, lustre and unique aroma. For home storage, it's recommended to keep them in dry tins. Put the drying agent in the tea tin after putting in tea leaves and then seal it with double deck lids. The tea leaves and agent are not mixed together. Finally cover it with fresh-keeping bag and store it in the refrigerator. In this way, the tea can preserve its quality for a year.

For Oolong tea

2. Black tea and Oolong: These are easy to store because they are slow to decay or age. They can maintain their quality for a fairly long time if kept away from sunlight, high temperature and peculiar smells.

For scented tea

3. Scented tea: A reprocessed tea from green tea can easily decay because of its high water content. Moisture protection is emphasized during
its storage. Try to store it in a cool and dry environment free from peculiar
smells. It doesn't necessarily need to be kept in the absence of light. Therefore, it can be placed in nice glass bottles for appreciation.

4. Pu'er tea: If preserved well, its aroma grows stronger with aging. Mix old tea with fresh tea in an earthen jar to accelerate the aging process. To drink the cake tea, break the whole pieces into loose tea and place them in a jar.

For Pu'er tea

Tea soothes the mind and soul.

EPILOGUE

My Zen of Tea

Many western people study the Oriental culture at my studio. Normally, they are senior managers of multi-national companies, university scholars as well as charming wives. They need to know China better for business, career, family life or they simply have an interest in the culture. Our systematic courses include the experiential module of tea, which can be divided into the four scopes of art, social custom and etiquette, classic history, and the latest developments. One of my students, a business man, told me that wherever he went on the trip around China he was always surrounded by too many wine glasses filled with alcoholic drinks stronger than whisky, brandy and vodka. The endless amount of hard drink, which could bring on a headache and stomachache, were unwelcome to him. However, many local people kept doing this until he was dead drunk. I suggested that he just raise a cup of tea with grace, and say (pronounce) *"yi cha dai jiu"* at the moment. On hearing this, not only will the hosts stop urging you to drink more, but also they think highly of you as an old China hand. Learning tea etiquette in advance is an effective way to extend your friendship with the Chinese.

Growing up in the scents of books and tea, I studied traditional arts since childhood like the practice of Tongzi Gong in Kung Fu. This helped me learn the Chinese Tao of Tea quickly and became an expert of it later. Before receiving my master's degree from Peking University, I had already received the highest-grade tea master rank for winning a series of championship of official tea art competitions. I decided to build up a research-led studio aiming to preserve and carry forward the heritage of the art of Chinese tea.

Recognized as one of the top tea masters, I am often asked what this title means. When asked, I tell a true story from the Ming dynasty written by a man of great learning named Zhang Dai (1597-1679).

"I (Zhang Dai) went to visit a famous tea master named Min Wenshui in Huizhou District. He didn't come back till midnight. After a short conversation, Mr. Min rose suddenly, finding an excuse to leave again. I kept waiting for him to come back.

"Before dawn, Min was back and stared at me, saying, 'Are you still here?'

"'Yes, I've heard about you so long, and wish to have a drink with you before I go,' I said.

"Mr. Min was pleased. He prepared the tea himself. When it was ready, he led me into a room, where everything was neat and tidy, and decorated by rare and precious tea utensils.

"Under the lamp light, I observed the color of the liquor, 'What is this tea?'

"'Langyuan (famous ancient tea produced in Sichuan Province).'

"I tasted it and said, 'Don't deceive me. Though the method of production is Langyuan, the leaves are not.'

"'What is it then?' asked Min with a smile.

"After tasting it one more time, I replied, 'why is it so much like Luojie Tea (produced in Zhejiang Province)?'

"Mr. Min was quite struck by my answer.

"The topic then turned to the water. I didn't think it was Hui Spring (located in Wuxi of Jiangsu Province) as Min told me. 'Don't try to make fun of me. How can Hui Spring water still retain its keenness after being carried here over a long distance?' I said to him.

"Min finally agreed to tell me the secret. Again he took another teapot, and asked me to try it.

"'Well, its fragrance is strong, and its flavor is very mild. This must be a spring picked tea, while the one we just had was an autumn tea,' I said.

"Mr. Min burst into laughter and said, 'Marvelous! I'm a man of seventy,

A photo taken on the way to the mountain area of Sichuan Province, Southwest China, for collecting folk tea culture

yet I have never met a tea connoisseur like you.' As a result, we became fast friends."

My students often feel this story is inconceivable. To prove it, I give them a spot demonstration. With my eyes closed, I smell a row of empty cups in front of me one by one. The students keep the tea liquor hidden somewhere else. After that, I can name each tea in order, and tell where they were produced, when they were picked, how they were processed, the quality and grades, and what kind of small mistakes the students made when they brewed it. "Yun (my first name in Chinese, pronounced like 'Win' in Mandarin) won again! Awesome! Master *Shifu*." It often draws a chorus of ooohh and aaahhh. They are all astonished at my comment, as if I had participated in the collection, stir-frying, purchasing and infusion of those teas.

It actually takes a lot of painstaking efforts to become an expert of tea, similar to learning Kung Fu. In the beginning, I needed to practice everything, including lute-playing and Chinese classical dance, calligraphy, painting, knowledge of antique, art of flower arrangement, costume design, and drama performance. Also I have trudged through mountain roads in the territories of poisonous mosquitoes and snakes to take pictures and collect ecological tea customs by myself. I've even fallen from the back of a horse, which was scared by the beast-roaring. With perseverance, all my efforts have paid off.

After I began to teach westerners about Chinese culture such as the

The theory of today's pressure deduction has its root in the Chinese Tao of tea.

Chinese Tao of Tea, calligraphy, Tai-Chi, Beijing Opera appreciation, I realized that only if we had the scope and thinking of the multivariate world, could we treasure the culture of our own with more sense and sensibility.

I'd emphasize that tea drinking is like a spa or yoga for the soul at any time. We moderns care too much about appearances, rather than the inner beauty. However, tea can be a life style or a friend for Zen meditation.

The ancient Chinese didn't mean to make drinking tea so complicated. The reason is that the Chinese Tao of Tea trains you to control your heart. Therefore, the theory of today's pressure deduction course has its roots in the Chinese Tao of Tea. There are rules and procedures for the sommeliers in their gestures and utensils that they use in boiling water and infusing tea, as well as for the guests in the appreciation of tea. It starts from the heart, and ends at the tips of the fingers. Look at the stream of water moistening the tea leaves under your hands. It is the very environment, atmosphere and procedures in the ceremonies that help the participants lay down their earthly troubles bit by bit. The appreciation not only requires the look of the tea leaves themselves, but the excellent combination of their color, aroma, taste and form. The perfection and refinement of the tea master and even the artistic beauty of the tea utensils can also play a role in entertaining the senses so as to achieve harmony between the body and soul.

Silent, pleasant, simple and beautiful is the Zen portrait of your feeling during this moment. Since introduced to Japan, the Chinese Tao of Tea has become one of the required courses for the samurais. The tranquility in the tea room can soothe their soul and free them for a brief moment from the fighting and killing of the battlefield. Consequently, calmly taking a bowl of tea has become an indispensable part of their daily life.

Tea drinking is like a spa or yoga for your body and soul at anytime, anywhere.

At times, we struggle with the fast pace of modern times, hustling at work with our fierce competition. However, things don't always work out the way you planned them. We work and socialize everyday with a seemingly decent look, but we return home exhausted with the brouhaha still reverberating at our ears. Accordingly your mind is filled with anxiety and worries. Your stomach feels a dull pain. Just like the Lynette in *Desperate Housewives*, with golden acupuncture needles inserted in her head, and tranquillizer pills taken, the horrible headache still sticks to her like a shadow following ceaselessly. At such moments, tea will help you to regain the inner peace. When the tea is served, its fragrance relaxes your body and calms your mind. Under the moonlight with gentle breezes blowing through the perennial pine trees and ever straight bamboos, the boiling water for tea brewing carries you away to the serene rivers and lakes and up to mountain tops and the sky. You can feel the vigor and vitality of nature with a completely open mind. At the end, you'll forget the outside world, reaching a harmony between heaven and man. All your anger will be left behind. Then there is a moment for you to think more about the saying that reflects the spirit of the Chinese Tao of Tea: "Yesterday is history,

Tea, as well as Chinese classic furniture and ceremics, is a carrier of the art of Oriental life.

tomorrow is a mystery, but today is a gift. That is why we call it present."

This is the health benefit that the Chinese Tao of Tea brings to humanity. If you allow fury and indignation to fill your heart, you will often lose more than what you gain from your indulgences. It is because impetuousness keeps your mind in rage and narrowness. Medically speaking, the continuous rage could change your internal secretion and lead to ailments like high blood pressure and heart diseases. As the great French writer Hugo said, "The vastest on the earth is the ocean, vaster than the ocean is the sky, yet vaster than the sky is the broad human vision." Tea is a mirror of the soul.

In a large city built upon reinforced concrete, in the commercial age full of impetuousness, and in the day by day bustle among the abundance of official documents and on the tight schedule, I have found from the Chinese Tao of Tea the long-missing balance between body and mind, the elusive tranquility, and the secret for keeping beauty, energy and youthfulness. A cup of tea a day, keeps the aging away.

In closing, I wish to deeply thank Mr. Le Yan (Roy) and Ms. Mao Xianzhi for supporting me in both overcoming a lot of hardships during the Chinese Tao of Tea learning and writing this book. Special thanks to Mr. Wu Jiaxuan, the Ambassador Extraordinary and Plenipotentiary of the PRC to Jamaica, and his wife. Uncle Wu's father Mr. Wu Juenong (1897-1989), the former Vice Minister of Agriculture of China, had devoted himself to the vitalization of Chinese tea industry. In addition, I also feel obliged to the China Red Sandal Wood Museum, as well as to Guanfu Classic Art Museum for providing me pictures of their precious collection.

When an artist of the Chinese Tao of Tea puts down the tea utensils, not only the artist herself, but also the guests will feel reluctant to leave as if parting with their sweetheart. Many have fallen in love with Chinese tea. When will the West understand the 5,000-year Chinese Tao of Tea? Maybe it is the high time. It will exceed your expectations. Hope my pen and lens will attract you to start enjoying tea and learning more about Oriental wisdom.

APPENDICES
Bibliography

1. Laozi (Lao-tzu), *Dao De Jing (Tao Te Ching)*, Shanxi Guji Press, 2000

2. Kongzi (Confucius), *Analects of Confucius (Lun Yu)*, Shanxi Guji Press, 1999

3. Sun-tzi, *The Art of War*, Shanghai Guji Press, 2006

4. Huineng, *The Sixth Zen Patriarch's Dharma Jewel Platform Sutra (Liuzu Tanjing)*, Jiangsu Guji Press, 2002

5. Lu Yu, *The Classic of Tea*, Zhejiang Guji Press, 2004

6. Wu Juenong, *Review to The Classic of Tea*, China Agriculture Press, 2005

7. Luo Guanzhong, *The Romance of Three Kingdom*, Tianjing Guji Press, 1997

8. Kakuzo Okakura, *The Book of Tea*, Charles E. Tuttle, 1998

9. William H. Ukers, *All about tea*, The Tea and Coffee Trade Journal Company, 1935

10. Wang Shixiang (Wang, Shih-hsiang), Yuan Quanyou, *Classic Chinese Furniture*, Tenth Union International Inc, 1997

11.Zhu Jiajin, *The Forbidden City Treasure*, The Forbidden City Press, 2007

12. Chen Lihua, *Li Zhi Hua Tang (China Red Sandal Wood Museum)*, Wenwu Press, 2007

13. Yu Yanyan, *Chinese Tea Sets through The Ages*, Zhejiang Photography Press, 2001

14. Liang Sicheng, *A Pictorial History of Chinese Architecture*, China Architecture Industry Press, 1991

15. Ma Weidu, *Classical Chinese Doors & Windows*, China Architecture Industry Press, 2006

INDEX

...ty	2070 BC – 1600 BC
...ty	1600 BC – 1046 BC
...n Period	1046 BC – 256 BC
...eriod	1046 BC – 771 BC
	770 BC – 256 BC
	770 BC – 476 BC
	475 BC – 221 BC
...asty	221 BC – 206 BC
...asty	206 BC – 220 AD
	206 BC – 25 AD
	25 AD – 220 AD
...ynasty	220 AD – 280 AD
...ynasty	220 AD – 265 AD
Southern Dynasties	221 AD – 263 AD
...nasties	222 AD – 280 AD
...ynasties	265 AD – 420 AD
	265 AD – 316 AD
	317 AD – 420 AD
...ty	420 AD – 589 AD
...ies and Ten States	420 AD – 589 AD
...asties	439 AD – 581 AD
...es	581 AD – 618 AD
...asty	618 AD – 907 AD
...n Song Dynasty	907 AD – 960 AD
...n Song Dynasty	907 AD – 960 AD
...nasty	902 AD – 979 AD
...asty	960 AD – 1279
...ynasty	960 AD – 1127
...Dynasty	1127 – 1279
...Dynasty	916 AD – 1125
...Dynasty	1115 – 1234
	1038 – 1227
	1279 – 1368
	1368 – 1644
	1644 – 1911